# The Study
# Skills Guide

D0061110

# The Study Skills Guide

Essential strategies
for smart students

Jacqueline Connelly
and Patrick Forsyth

KoganPage

LONDON PHILADELPHIA NEW DELHI

**Publisher's note**

Every possible effort has been made to ensure that the information contained in this book is accurate at the time of going to press, and the publishers and authors cannot accept responsibility for any errors or omissions, however caused. No responsibility for loss or damage occasioned to any person acting, or refraining from action, as a result of the material in this publication can be accepted by the editor, the publisher or either of the authors.

First published in Great Britain and the United States in 2010 by Kogan Page Limited

Apart from any fair dealing for the purposes of research or private study, or criticism or review, as permitted under the Copyright, Designs and Patents Act 1988, this publication may only be reproduced, stored or transmitted, in any form or by any means, with the prior permission in writing of the publishers, or in the case of reprographic reproduction in accordance with the terms and licences issued by the CLA. Enquiries concerning reproduction outside these terms should be sent to the publishers at the undermentioned addresses:

120 Pentonville Road
London N1 9JN
United Kingdom
www.koganpage.com

525 South 4th Street, #241
Philadelphia PA 19147
USA

4737/23 Ansari Road
Daryaganj
New Delhi 110002
India

© Jacqueline Connelly and Patrick Forsyth, 2010

The right of Jacqueline Connelly and Patrick Forsyth to be identified as the authors of this work has been asserted by them in accordance with the Copyright, Designs and Patents Act 1988.

ISBN     978 0 7494 6126 3
E-ISBN   978 0 7494 6127 0

**British Library Cataloguing-in-Publication Data**

A CIP record for this book is available from the British Library.

**Library of Congress Cataloging-in-Publication Data**

Forsyth, Patrick B.
   The study skills guide : essential strategies for smart students / Patrick Forsyth, Jacqueline Connelly.
      p. cm.
   Includes bibliographical references and index.
   ISBN 978-0-7494-6126-3 – ISBN 978-0-7494-6127-0 (ebook)   1. Study skills–Handbooks, manuals, etc.   2. College students–Handbooks, manuals, etc.   I. Connelly, Jacqueline. II. Title.
   LB2395.F66 2010
   378.1'70281–dc22

                                                                2010027803

Typeset by Graphicraft Limited, Hong Kong
Production managed by Jellyfish
Printed in the UK by CPI Antony Rowe

*For Fabian and Tilly*
*– one day this may be useful to you too.*

# CONTENTS

Tables 1.1, 2.1, 2.2, 6.1, 7.4 and 8.4 are available as downloadable Word documents on the Kogan Page website.

To access, go to www.koganpage.com/TheStudySkillsGuide and enter the password: SSG1926

# FOREWORD

I was the first member of my family to go to university and so absolutely everything about the experience was brand new to me. I had no parents, brothers, sisters, cousins, uncles, aunts or grandparents who could pass on any story about how many essays they had written, how many books they pretended to read, how many nights they had spent in the Student Union bar. I had to find out the whole thing for myself, and I quickly became so deeply hooked on the whole experience that I found I could not escape it and have never yet tried. Of course, you can easily accuse me of being a geek. I was fascinated by my undergraduate modules and really enjoyed the voyage of exploration I undertook with them. But, as well as my intellectual outlook, it also transformed my life in many other ways, for instance creating bonds with a variety of people that have endured over the years. To give a quick example, recently I had a special celebratory lunch with two friends marking the anniversary of our first meeting as undergraduates 20 years earlier. University is an experience not to be missed, but getting the best out of it can be tricky. Too often there is the temptation to overindulge on the social side to the detriment of the academic. In part, this can be caused by a failure to engage with the new academic demands university makes. This book is aimed at helping you deal with just those demands.

Going to university is an exciting and challenging experience. You will make a transformation into a world that can seem very strange and different when first encountered. For some it will mean not only coming to grips with new ways of learning, but also living apart from parents, family or friends for the first time. The good thing is that universities are very welcoming and are very much aware that the brand-new undergraduate, regardless of previous experience and background, needs plenty of support and help. You will find that support at both the central and departmental level.

Every university expects new students to be somewhat confused when they first arrive and so are fully prepared for a list of questions ranging from 'where can I buy a new kettle?' to 'how can I get hold of the recommended texts on my reading list?' Indeed, so attuned are universities to the need to ease the initial introduction that when new undergraduates arrive, they tend to be subjected to a veritable deluge of information. After a while, the brain often stops processing all this new material and too much information and advice can seem as daunting as too little. This too is understood, and so the key things to remember about first arrival at university are that questions are there to be asked, there is no such thing as a silly question when everything around you is so new, no one minds repeating themselves, and you should never feel afraid to ask for help.

Another startling revelation about university life is the vast range of extra-curricula activities it can offer you. There are tons of Student Union societies dedicated to every kind of sporting, cultural, political and religious/spiritual activity. They will often offer as much novelty as your studies themselves. These kinds of activities provide a fantastically vibrant culture which can frame your university experience around the central act of studying for a degree, and in some cases link directly and usefully to it.

In this welter of new experiences, it is often easy to feel that things are passing you by, or that you are not connecting with your studies or fellow students as easily as others. This is also something which is very much 'par for the course' in the first year. Nearly all universities structure their programmes to reflect the inexperience of first year students, which means that degrees are often weighted towards second and third year study. This helps you build upon your previous studies and reorient yourself. Very few people make the transition seamlessly, and as you make the adjustment, aided by the various support networks run by your university, you will begin to realize that you have changed a good deal, too. Confidence will grow during the course of the first year, which often means that you can feel a completely different person by the second. The novelist Evelyn Waugh felt this process and commented in *Brideshead Revisited* that 'it was normal to spend one's second year shaking off the friends of one's first'. This is not to say that you won't make lasting and enduring friendships during your first year (!), only that you will probably enter the second year feeling that you have emerged from a period of great change.

A crucial part of the transition is adjusting to the new intellectual challenges thrown down by your studies. As noted, universities are very good at providing a plethora of study support. Most institutions have dedicated teams offering generic study skills with classes in things such as note taking, essay writing and presentations. These are often complemented by more subject-specific programmes in your home department.

This book has been designed to work with those systems and act as a handy and constant summarizer, interpreter and guide. The aim of the book is not to overwhelm you with detail and overly rigid rules, but to provide essential useful hints, thoughts and suggested approaches to study in order to turn what might seem daunting demands into a manageable process. Its contents encapsulate the essentials and are based on the observation of the experiences of many students, the questions regularly asked by students and specific enquiries made of students as this book was written. Your studies should be challenging and demanding, but they should also be hugely stimulating and rewarding. An enormous part of the fun of university life is the immersion in your degree subject, and this book has been designed to help you in that immersion in order to get the best out of your studies.

I could end by wishing you good luck, though the contents that follow make amply clear that success is much more than a matter of luck, so I wish you well. If you remember that how it all goes is largely down to you and act accordingly, then it will go well.

*Mark Connelly*
*Professor of Modern British History,*
*University of Kent*

---

Note: the authors wish to thank Mark Connelly, not only for writing this foreword, but also for help throughout the writing of this book. His experience, and his experience working with many students currently and in the past, has informed the project throughout and allowed it to reflect the real questions and concerns typically expressed by students getting to grips with the university environment and the challenge ahead of them.

# THANKS

The author of many books, I have worked successfully in collaboration with a number of writers in the past; it can be something that requires effort and organization for both those involved. But this title was special. As the lead author of a co-authored work, I can say that this is one small section on which there has been no collaboration whatsoever.

So, having already thanked Mark Connelly earlier, let me now thank my co-author, Jacqueline Connelly, for her involvement in this project. I may have set the project up, but she made it possible; she worked tirelessly to complete her part of the writing and did so against a tight deadline to ensure that publication was possible at the start of the academic year. More than this, she brought invaluable experience, knowledge and insight to the content. Her direct university experience, both as a student and as a manager, literally saw this book to fruition and ensured that it truly addresses the real student experience.

Along the way her patience in face of my impatience and her nit-picking attention to university workings and terminology made her an admirable collaborator. Thank you so much Jacqui – what shall we write next?

*Patrick Forsyth*

# Introduction: destination graduation

**In this chapter...**

Here we consider the **nature of the change** that going into higher education makes, the reasons for doing it and the opportunities it presents you with, both for the time spent on it and thereafter. It also begins to look at how your success will be affected by how you work; and shows how this book can help, though remember what Vidal Sassoon is reputed to have said: 'The only place where success comes before work is in the dictionary.'

If you are reading this you have probably just taken a big step: you have left school behind and moved into higher education. However you got there, and it may not have been straight from school (maybe you are going back to education as a mature student in mid-career or after a spell in work), it is doubtless an achievement. You got the necessary results and you were accepted onto a course at a higher education institution with the intention of getting a formal qualification.

## Big changes

Make no mistake, life is now going to change and maybe change radically. University or college is not like school. Certainly it is much less regimented and there is less supervision and that may sound good, but it leaves much more down to you. Consider the details.

University is a different world from the previous study you will have done at school or college. As we will mention elsewhere in this book, university is not 'seventh form', it is not the same kind of step as year to year at school; it is a fundamentally different form of study. The earlier you appreciate this the earlier you can get to grips with what will be required of you on your course.

There are practical differences, of course:

| School/College | University |
| --- | --- |
| Free (if state school) | Fee paying |
| Living with parents | Living independently (if studying away from home) |
| Legal requirement till 16 | Attendance voluntary. Chasing of non-attendees will be minimal |
| More decisions made for you | More independence and responsibility for own progress |

All these differences are important, but the ones we want to emphasize here are those related to the nature of the work you will do. Of course, these will vary by course, university and individual circumstances, but are likely to include:

| School/College | University |
| --- | --- |
| Timetable planned for you, and your time filled | Contact hours minimal; you need to plan your private study |
| More frequent and shorter pieces of coursework which are closely linked to ongoing lessons | Longer pieces of coursework, with deadlines set early in course, spaced more widely and not necessarily linked to current topics |
| Directed teaching – narrower range of material for more focused learning. Fixed curriculum. Learning environment prescribed | Interpretive teaching – need to manipulate a broader range of facts and material to create sophisticated arguments. Will not be spoon-fed answers or the way to present them |

University is like membership of an exclusive gym or health club; to get the most out of it you can't just sign up, you need to go and make full use of all the facilities.

That said, you need to adapt to new ways of working, fit with new systems and procedures and find ways of doing so that meet the need and yet suit you. There may well be other significant changes that go with the move. Many people move to a new area, many find themselves living away from home for the first time and some find all that takes a bit of getting used to. So be it. Things are going to be different and such tasks as finding somewhere to live and sorting your finances all take time. You may be juggling university work with family commitments.

But most people find all this readjustment eminently worthwhile. It is a stage when your whole way of life changes: new places, new people and new things to do, and above all a new freedom – the period ahead should be interesting, it should be enjoyable and it puts you on a path which can potentially influence literally the rest of your life – enabling you to start to fulfil your ambitions and carve out the future life you want.

# Exciting opportunities

You may face changes, but you are also presented with a major opportunity. Yes, major: higher education is the life and career equivalent of an open goal. But it does not just happen; you must make the most of it. Opportunities need grasping. In this book we focus not so much on making your next few years fun (though there is every reason why they should be just that) but rather on helping you ensure that you can tackle the work element in a way that is manageable, stress free and most likely to ensure that you succeed in getting the result you want and enjoy all the wider opportunities that university/college offers. Note: while there is a whole range of institutions, ranging from a variety of colleges to, say, business schools, at which readers may be studying, the word 'university' is used here to include them all.

And here is a key question to ask: will you graduate successfully and with the degree classification that you want?

There is every likelihood that you will; but only if you get to grips with, and work with, a new situation. Doing so requires understanding, consideration and application; true enough, but this makes the process sound like hard work and surely your course itself will be hard work enough. This book aims to streamline the process of getting to grips with the new ways in which you will have to work: to kick-start you into a new, effective and appropriate way of working that will help you enjoy what you do and increase your chances of success both day by day and in terms of your ultimate graduation. This applies whatever the nature of what you study. You may be studying to:

- Obtain a non-vocational qualification; for instance subjects such as business administration or marketing could take you into a wide range of business careers. Indeed, your chosen subject may, at this stage, be more general still and linking it to a specific career choice may be another decision to be made over the next few years.

- Obtain a vocational or professional qualification, perhaps one linked to a specific career choice already made. To be a doctor, a research scientist, computer designer or whatever may necessitate particular qualifications being obtained. Doing so is simply a given if you are to pursue your chosen path.

The approaches reviewed here – concerned with both what you need to do and how you can best tackle it – are also designed to fit with the multifaceted nature of life working towards qualifications. Thus Chapter 6, for example, which is concerned with writing essays, dissertations and more, is not only concerned to spell out practical ways of delivering a final text that will get you marked high, it also shows how to do so efficiently to make best use of your time: to write better, and more quickly. This is important. There will be many calls on your time: lectures, classes, tutorials and more – and you doubtless want a social life too.

Getting on top of the process is vital. Keep up to date, maximize the use of your time, work in an effective and disciplined way and you will work successfully and have time for the other things you want to do. Get behind or waste time and catching up becomes difficult, achieving the results you want becomes less likely and the problem escalates as time available to catch up is limited; there will also be a real clash between work and your social or home life.

# Life after university

There is a further point to keep in mind here. The world, and the world of work specifically, has changed a great deal in the first years of the current century. It is a safe prediction that it will change more and is likely to change more quickly.

The world of work is dynamic and competitive. Employers have had to contend with volatile economies and operating conditions. In the commercial sector competition for jobs (and promotion) is as fierce as it has ever been. Organizations succeed only if their employees have the necessary skills and experience and perform well at whatever they may do. They know this. Thus careful recruitment and selection are regarded as vital, not least because employment legislation has made mistakes (employing someone who proves inadequate and must be replaced) an expensive and time-consuming process to correct.

All this means that even those with the highest qualifications do not necessarily just walk straight out of higher education into the job they want. Sadly, you are unlikely to work magic just by snapping your fingers and saying 'Hire me'. You will need to work at the job-seeking process in due course too, and at ongoing career management. Thus every aspect of your record during higher education can help create for you a profile that appeals to employers. You want to gain the qualification you aim at, you want to achieve that with an impressive record of how you have spent the time leading up to it, and you want to do all this in a manageable way that allows you to benefit from and enjoy the whole process.

This book aims to smooth the path. Whether you are just starting, or indeed are a little way down the track, the lessons here can assist you in achieving what you want, and increase the likelihood that you can excel.

## How to use this book

To get the best from reading this book it is worth keeping pen and paper close at hand:

- Note when anything mentioned seems to have direct application for you.

- Specify specific action you will take (even if this is simply to consider something further).

- Watch for 'Action' boxes within the text; these are designed to help point the way, creating links to your own situation.

- Use the 'Your notes' pages at the end of each chapter. These provide space for you to add your own notes.

- Make the book 'yours'; that is, by adding notes, coupled perhaps with highlighting key parts of the text, turn the book into your personal guide to the task ahead, one that will be useful throughout your course.

Act now!

Be warned: time starts to go quickly at this stage of life, and for those in further education there are many distractions, some constructive, others not. There is a line written by John Lennon which says that life is what happens while you are busy making other plans. It's a sobering thought. It is all too easy to find that you are a substantial way through your chosen course and lagging behind what you intended, indeed emergency remedial action midway can – even if it is effective – rapidly dilute the satisfaction to be gained from the whole process. A little time spent now will ensure that your first thought on graduation day does not start with the words, 'If only...'.

> ### Read on
>
> Having set the scene, let's see how you can work smarter, not harder.
> The next chapter shows you how to make best use of your time;
> productivity is a foundation to making your work lead to good results.

## Your notes

........................................................................................

........................................................................................

........................................................................................

........................................................................................

........................................................................................

........................................................................................

........................................................................................

........................................................................................

........................................................................................

........................................................................................

........................................................................................

........................................................................................

........................................................................................

........................................................................................

........................................................................................

........................................................................................

........................................................................................

........................................................................................

........................................................................................

........................................................................................

........................................................................................

# 01
# Managing your time

**In this chapter...**

Here we look at **productivity**. Sounds daunting? It just means being sure that you use your time efficiently so that you maximize the effectiveness of what you do. It means avoiding certain pitfalls, establishing the right habits (which make it easy to keep up good practice) and being conscious of time as a resource that needs organizing. Make no mistake: being well organized in this way gives you an immediate edge in seeking good results. Busy times lie ahead and, as Jonathan Lazear put it, 'Tomorrow is always the busiest day of the week.'

## Manage your time effectively

Whatever else you may experience over the time you are studying, you are likely to be busy. Indeed, fitting everything in can be a problem. Look around you; you will notice that some people always seem to manage their time better than others. Like so much else, this does not just happen. And it is without doubt one of the key factors governing success in studying, indeed its relevance continues on – it's a career skill. If two people have the same ability and, all other things being equal (which they are not, of course, but the point remains), and one manages their time better than the other, then they may well also make better progress. Managing your time effectively not only allows you to be more productive, doing more as well as being able to concentrate on the priority tasks and get better results, it will most likely be noticed; it labels you as an achiever. We are not suggesting that you set out to be teacher's pet in any unpleasant sense, but there is no harm in being seen to be taking your course seriously. Cooperation is a two-way street and teachers are likely to put themselves out more for those who appear keen rather than bolshie.

This is perhaps the classic area of good intentions. Everyone says they are going to manage their time well; but it can be easier said than done – time management is about self-management and therefore about self-discipline. This may sound daunting, but good practice quickly becomes a habit and, as such, while it may take effort to acquire, the whole process does then become easier once you have made a commitment and done some groundwork.

# The problem

On the one hand you have a fair period of time stretching ahead of you as you start a course, one numbered in years. On the other hand the conflict of priorities is serious; you may:

- early on, have time taken up with settling in, finding accommodation and simply getting used to a new way of life and all it entails;
- need to do some paid work alongside your course, either to keep you solvent or to extend your spending power;
- have major subsidiary activities and objectives that take time alongside your studying; these could range from athletics to theatre;
- commute and take up time 'on the road' as it were, if you do not live on campus or nearby.

Beyond all this you will have other interests and friends all demanding some time if you are to get the best out of the whole experience. Some of this is constructive, necessary and useful. Some things are just fun – and can range from a formal function like a wedding to a comprehensive investigation of the real ale sold within a five-mile radius. But given the pressures, how do you get everything done?

# The key principles

What are the key principles? (Here we touch on only the essentials; but it is a topic worth some separate study.) Consider the following sequence of action:

- First, you must plan to plan. You need a system, and it can be a loose-leaf diary or notebook rather than a generic system, but it must allow you to note what you have on the go, to prioritize it and to progress it. Few people can truly hold everything necessary in their memory, though some claim to do so: realistically, therefore, some record in writing (or on an electronic system, of course) is always necessary.

- The second rule is to update your plan regularly. How long this takes will depend on exactly what you have to do. For the majority of people no more than five minutes will be necessary each day or even every few days. When you do this is a matter of personal preference – but it helps to do it regularly and maybe to do it at a regular time.

So far so good, and now the next step – you simply have to do what the plan says!

Doing it, of course, is where it all tends to become somewhat difficult. So many things conspire to stop you following your plan and it is here that the classic time wasters need controlling: too much time in unproductive activities, too many interruptions, and an ever-present clash with social life. You can – must – work at all of these, but two things especially need watching, which you can control:

- Putting off what you dislike or find difficult – it is constantly thinking about a task, shuffling papers, but coming to no conclusion or action that wastes so much time.

- Spending too much time on the things you like, and this often means the things that are less directly geared to core study issues. This is often the worse of the two problems.

## Action

Once you are into your new way of life, it may even be worth keeping a time log for a while. Just make a few notes. It is always a sobering exercise; try it for a couple of weeks and you will soon see where time goes. Almost always a log produces surprises: some things take up very much more time than you think they do. If you know how you work and what happens to your time, you can work at the details that will make you more productive.

In a sense, it really is true to say, 'That's all there is to it.' Time management may be a struggle to get organized, but the principles are, for the most part, common sense. Two final points:

- Do not think that because much of what needs doing cannot be planned (perhaps because it is reactive to things as they occur), you cannot manage it. You must plan the non-reactive time, and the less you have of it the more important it is to utilize it effectively.

- And consider the old maxim that there never seems to be time to do something properly but there always has to be time to do something again. Regularly you will find that to sort something may take half an hour or an hour instead of 10 minutes to do it right in the first place. The temptation is to get it done and out of the way, rather than pause and take longer, perhaps creating a new, sensible methodology that can be repeated. Take that time once, however, and you may save five minutes every day in future. That may not sound much, but it can mount up in a whole term or year (actually saving five minutes a day can save some 30 hours – some three working days!).

This is a most important area. Unless you get to grips with it you will be at a serious disadvantage alongside those who do. Become a master of your time and you become able to be more effective, both your results and the way you are seen will improve and this is one more aid to your achieving what you want.

# Never forget commitments

Soon after getting into your course you may well become convinced that a tutor has an infallible memory or uses something akin to magic to chivvy you for things requested almost in passing. They never seem to forget anything.

This is a good characteristic to find in a teacher and it is a good one for you to display to a teacher. Reliability is approved, it is efficient – knowing something will be as planned may be important – and it keeps the majority of contacts you have with all those in authority positive. You do not want their automatic recall of you to be of the endless chasers which they have had to make but which they regard as unnecessary.

Those that put you in mind of magic doubtless just have a good system. They have a dedicated page in a loose-leaf diary for each student with whom they work, and they keep a record of your projects large and small linked to their system and diary. If you make clear notes and monitor them regularly it works well, and if you build up the reputation of always honouring commitments, whichever way round, that will work well for you too.

---

**Action**

You will find that, whatever diary system you use, you will manage your time best if you plan your time rather than just list events, that is, lectures, meetings and so on. Block out activity time to research or write that essay. And do put in social engagements and commitments too where possible; though realistically only certain kinds of social activity can be planned, of course, including what you can does help the whole process. In this way all of your time can be monitored at a glance.

There is probably no such thing as a typical diary page. It will vary by individual, by what is being studied and by the time of year (for instance, the period leading up to examinations or tests may be very untypical). Some courses may have significant hours of hands-on tuition involved; computer courses of various sorts are one such. Others have significant amounts of informal and unscheduled work that must be done – reading for instance.

Some of the things that should appear in your diary and which most students will find valuable to schedule include:

- lectures and seminars (with specific timing and duration);
- other group discussion sessions;
- individual time with lecturers/tutors;
- hands-on practical work;
- preparation for and follow-up from lectures and seminars, including preparation of presentations;
- preparing and (separately) writing essays and other written material;
- reading;
- field visits and trips;
- research in all its forms;
- informal study collaboration, for example with other students;
- and ultimately, revision and examinations.

In addition, you may want to schedule a variety of non-study activities, some of which are closely linked to study work and some that are not, though they take time and work may need fitting around them. Examples here might include:

- attendance at student societies or on committees;
- social events (eg a wedding), especially if attending involves travel;
- personal administration (you might schedule an hour each month to sort your finances, for instance);
- any paid work being done;
- socializing – of a form where the time, formality or the closeness to work commitments makes putting it in your diary useful.

Clarity about any of these things that apply to you will help you keep organized and fit more in – in terms of work and play.

Keeping reasonably up to date and never having to pitch into sorting out a real backlog makes for an easier life and allows you to deliver the quality necessary, for an essay perhaps; overall, doing so will save you time.

# Always hit deadlines

Although deadlines are commitments, timing is worth a word in its own right. You do not just need to remember and do what the commitment entails, but do it by when it was arranged. So an essay, say, must reflect the brief given and be handed in on time. Remember that a last-minute rush and delivery even a bit late makes you lose out in two ways: the quality of work suffers and so does your reputation for good work. It is said that there was never a deadline in history that was not negotiable. This may be true and there is certainly no merit in being pushed somehow into agreeing to a deadline that you cannot possibly meet. It may need negotiation, or at least discussion, though understand that ultimately the decision is not yours and that deadlines are set in light of a bigger picture than you can perhaps see.

Once set, however, a deadline – your deadline – takes on another characteristic: it becomes irrevocable. It can do your reputation nothing but good to be known as someone who takes deadlines seriously and manages to deliver on time. Once you have said, 'I will make sure you have it on Friday week' or something similar, people should know it will be done.

Always think through any task before agreeing to any particular timing. The more complex the task, the more important this is. Something may appear straightforward, but it is only when you reach stage four perhaps that complications set in and this needs to be anticipated and built into your estimate of how long it will take – no doubt amongst all the other things you have on your plate. Sometimes a confusing incidence of what might be called 'deadline abuse' can occur. For example, a teacher wants something on, let us say, 31 May, so they build in a safety factor and say they need it by 25 May. But students know that this is what happens, so it is accepted with the thought that there is always a week or so built in, and that 2/3 June will do. The more people are involved in this scenario the more rapidly it gets much more complicated – and the only thing you can be sure of is that there will be a muddle. Deadlines should be honestly stated and then dealt with accordingly – and with care.

Note: tailored systems are available to help too. Check the website for the institution you attend as these vary, but, for example, at Kent University you can obtain a system called ASK (Assignment Survival Kit), a computer-based method of charting your work to help you keep on schedule.

# First, second and next

First things first it is said. This is a reminder of another area, something that is very much part of time management, the simple matter of setting priorities. Simple may seem the wrong choice of word and, of course, priority setting is not necessarily easy, but must be done. But it is a simple fact of life that you can complete only one task at a time. First you do one thing (albeit this may be part of a greater total task) and then you do another, and another. Sometimes you have to pause in one thing to tackle something else. For example, you may be writing an essay and pause to check something online or in a library. For the moment, the pause becomes a priority and can lead to total disruption; you meet someone in the library and do not get back to the essay for hours. Busy people often spend a great deal of time in trying to achieve impossibilities. If you can do only one thing at a time (and you can) then you must decide which task takes priority. Of course, you may well be progressing a number of things at the same time and this must be built into your decisions.

Some things need more time spent on them than do others. It may be a priority just to check one fact. Doing so will take only a few minutes. A different task, like writing a longer document such as an essay, may well have a deadline but the work needs to be spread over a number of days. When things change, and you accept this and add a new priority, you need to reassess the overall picture. For example, with something promised complete on a set date, and if things you could not predict at the time interfere, then there are not so many options; you can:

- work harder, long into the evening perhaps;
- delay some other task;
- delay the deadline (which may mean getting the agreement of someone else and, come to think of it, is the least attractive option!).

The temptation is to struggle on trying to do far too much for a while and then end up with something, or several somethings, done inadequately – or done late.

It would be great if nothing unpredictable happened in your life and you were able to do – and complete – everything exactly as you wanted. But realistically this is simply not real life; changes do occur. Such need recognizing and must be dealt with; often this demands some change.

There is much talk these days of stress and the management of it; but stress is in reality a reaction to circumstances rather than what the circumstances themselves do to you. Clear intentions and clear objectives should make it easier to decide priorities, and a realistic attitude to how you arrange your work makes for greater overall effectiveness. Nothing is achieved just by panicking or sitting around and wondering what to do or wishing the priority decision did not have to be made. Concern and constructive thought about how to sort something are positive. Worry is negative. What do all these thoughts have to do with your situation as a student?

Rapid and clear decisions made about your priorities – a continual process for most busy students – will make you more effective. Clarity of thought and decisiveness are both qualities looked for by teachers and ultimately by employers. Learning to be philosophical about the things that cause stress, and concentrating your thinking on the practicalities of what will work best, will reduce worry and get more done. And the whole thrust of this section is to show how increased effectiveness, and the impression that it gives, improves your prospects and your results. It may help to categorize the priority of different tasks. List all the tasks that you need to do in the next term and rate them from 1 to 10; 1 being urgent and very important, 10 being the least urgent and important. When you have done this, put them into a simple table like the one below to help make your priorities clear.

**TABLE 1.1** Prioritizing tasks

| Urgent, very important (1–3) | Important but not urgent (4–7) | Neither urgent nor important (8–10) |
|---|---|---|
| eg Type up essay – due end of the week | eg Write up notes from seminar last week | eg Start reading for an essay due in 4 months |
| | | |
| | | |
| | | |
| | | |
| | | |

# All the difference

At this point let's look at an example to see just what a difference managing your time well can make. A simple situation demonstrates: imagine that students A and B have essays to write, let's say both accept and respond to the brief accurately, but only student A approaches every stage well.

| Student A | Student B |
|---|---|
| Full attendance of lectures, tutorials etc | Gaps mean more checking/research |
| Good note taking and filing | More time needed to sort/access source material |
| Effective research | Poor research = less appropriate information |
| Comprehensive reading of books/materials | Only reads core textbook |
| Essay planned before writing starts | Lack of planning leads to more time spent rewriting |
| Interruptions during writing minimized | Restarting after interruption disrupts flow |
| Draft carefully checked | Poor checking = more corrections later |
| Delivered on time | Running late = quality suffers |
| Project completed with no remedial action | Time spent redoing things skimped |

Student B takes some more time at every stage if things are not done right, and the effect is cumulative: an inadequacy at any stage increases the time needed for the essay project and it all mounts up. Ineffectiveness of this sort can easily lead to such a project taking 20 per cent more time – or more.

# Always on target

On many courses students find that there are more than just deadlines, there are targets. This applies to a range of things, from written work to practical projects.

The implications of this are very clear. Because you are significantly more likely to register as doing well if you are consistently hitting your targets (much more so than in a, perhaps apparently appealing, laissez-faire situation), you may want to consider:

- making sure that you understand and program in any such targets realistically; this is especially important as they are set for you and doubtless come in various forms;
- making sure that any such targets set are regularly reviewed, and are documented clearly in whatever reminder and diary system you may use.

This may seem like a chore, but it must be done and is even best regarded as motivational – most of us like to know that all is going well rather than just believing that it is.

# Do more than is expected of you

This seems an obviously good thing, and certainly there are derogatory remarks that conjure up the opposite – we talk for instance of people scraping through, just doing sufficient to get by. This latter is not the attitude that tends to produce the best results. So, delivering more than others expect is, not surprisingly, to be recommended.

This does not mean, however, that study work has to take over your life and that 'more' is produced as a result of excessive hours worked. Of course, many courses demand hard work and the hours needed must be put in. So, accepting that, you need to be sufficiently industrious to create the right results and the right image. Remember that just being busy, especially being chaotically busy because you are disorganized, does not lead automatically to the desired results. Do not confuse activity with achievement – doing the right things well, being productive and working smarter rather than simply harder is what will give you the best results and allow time for other things.

Probably the most important way to deliver more is to think more about things than is necessary to complete the task. For example, an essay may be delivered on time and well written; it may also be something that is well received. Yet writing it may have involved little more than going through the motions, and it may leave you with a completed assignment but no further forward in any other way. Some extra research or discussion along the way may allow you to deliver an essay that is beyond routine and to end up more knowledgeable and better fitted to tackle the next stage of your course.

The same principle applies to much smaller issues. Say you sit on a small committee, and you find that the Chair always produces and circulates in advance a detailed agenda. The complexity may not make this essential, but those present are likely to find it useful; they also like the fact that the person in the chair is helpfully doing just a little more than is strictly necessary. Being known to operate this way helps that person stay on top of things and be seen in the right light. It is a principle worth using.

# Be honest

It is said that honesty is the best policy but people are not always honest. For instance, research (in the UK) has shown that some 20 per cent of people applying for new jobs complete the necessary application forms dishonestly, and this does not just include minor embellishments. Some people will even claim to have degrees from universities which they have never attended. It happens; yet the longer someone pursues a dishonest line, the more vulnerable they become to discovery.

The truth of the matter is that while you may prosper by lying, you only have to get found out once and any good it may have done in the past is lost forever. In any case most people do want to achieve whatever they do on their own merits; there can surely be no real and lasting satisfaction in conning your way through. Here consider the time implications and what that leads to. For example, you have an essay to complete. You miss the deadline (perhaps only by a little), deliver something in part plagiarized from the internet and are dishonest in the face of criticism. If the essay must be rewritten then you will have taken up vastly more time than would have been necessary to do it in the first place. The fact that it was late, inadequate and your excuses were simply untrue hardly does you a service.

Note: In the light of real, unavoidable delay (such as serious illness or bereavement) your university should be able to help. In the first instance you should approach your lecturer and explain the circumstances as early and as fully as possible (even if you cannot do so in person). In many universities your information is considered, in confidence, by a panel that will make recommendations on how to proceed. Your university should provide all of the specific information on these procedures on its website or in course handbooks. If you can anticipate such difficulty it may be worth checking out in advance precisely how such things work.

Honesty is the best policy – those academics you are involved with should know that you are honest and keep your word; additionally, honesty links to trust which is an important factor too if you are to get the best from the overall teacher/student relationship. One additional point: always start as you mean to go on. For instance, when you first start your course, aim to make a positive impact fast, both in what you do and achieve and in how you are seen.

It is easy to have good intentions, but you need more than that. Only by thinking about your time, your priorities and how you do things will you be truly productive and able to deliver quality work. Whether you are working solo to write an essay or involved in a team on some project work, the implications are the same: get organized – you will save time and be more likely to maximize the quality of what you do.

## Action

It will help you move in the right direction if you visualize where time goes diagrammatically. First draw a simple pie-chart – see illustration – and divide it (estimate initially) into a number of appropriate sections, illustrating how you spend your time now. You may need a number of slices: sleeping, eating, socializing, working (and use subsections here: writing essays, research and so on as appropriate) to show where time goes now.

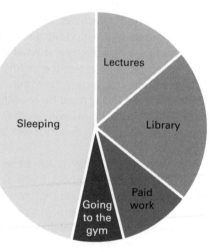

Now draw another illustrating how you feel it should look. Seeing any change you need to make in this way will help you bridge the gap.

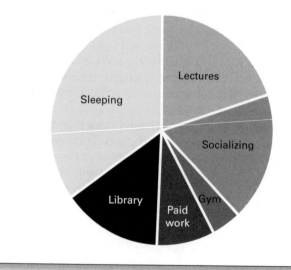

Now a final reminder of some key approaches:

---

**Top tips...**

### ...for saving time

As this chapter will have made clear, good management of time is in the detail. There is no single magic formula; many things help. This is not to negate other factors, but these are especially important:

1 Always devise and work from a plan (and make it in writing).

2 Consider priorities carefully and make good decisions about what to do first, second and so on.

3 Resist and deal with interruptions. Two kinds are most common:

   – those that come while you are working (on an essay perhaps);

   – those that come at random (like someone suggesting a drink after a lecture).

   Where necessary the best response is just to say 'No' (perhaps explaining or arranging an alternative time for something); collaboration amongst close groups is valuable too, a common approach helping you all get more done.

4 Be punctual and respect deadlines.

5 Spend time on organizing yourself to create routines and systems that then save you time on a regular basis.

6 Work wherever possible to your time clock (for instance, do not try to write an essay late into the night if you are a morning person, or vice versa).

7 Select good (productive) methods for tasks such as research. Examples occur throughout the text, for example a suggestion is made about organizing to write essays uninterrupted.

8 Be organized: don't waste time looking for things that you should be able to find in a moment.

9 Create a clear archive system – as well as being organized, make sure of the longer term; you must be able to find things filed a year ago.

10 Discipline yourself over computer procedure (even one piece of lost work/research can waste hours). So such things as:

   – saving written work on your computer on a memory stick too,

   – remembering to update anti-virus software regularly,

       – keeping e-mails manageable by deleting and categorizing them as appropriate,

all help ensure you avoid disaster.

11 Make notes, but remember that abbreviation will only save time if you can follow and interpret your notes later.

12 Keep notes on sources: what systems and which people can you return to because they help effectively.

13 Carry a notebook: university life is hectic and things may occur to you at any time of day in many circumstances.

14 Work with others: various collaborations are described in these pages – all can save time.

15 Assess the time effectiveness of things you do and work to instil the right habits and maintain initiatives that are productive.

Overall, remember that people who use time most effectively are not cleverer than you, they just keep time implications uppermost in their minds and work at being productive in what becomes a common-sense kind of way until it becomes second nature.

## Read on...

Having given attention to creating some useful time within an acceptable balance of work and play, we turn now to an activity that will necessarily demand a fair amount of time, though again its effectiveness is influenced by just how you go about it, and that's study.

# Your notes

# 02
# Effective study

**In this chapter...**

Now it's time to consider the **types of formal teaching** you will get at university, and how you can get the most out of each one. Lectures, seminars, practical classes and e-learning are all covered, as well as group project work, an increasingly common feature of many courses. All are important. As Lord Macaulay said: 'Knowledge advances by steps, not by leaps.' Finally we consider examinations; how to revise and prepare for them effectively, and how to manage your nerves.

Never confusing activity with achievement was a point made in the last chapter. Here we look at the need to go about your studies in the right way if you are to maximize the chances of your getting the best results. We look at each of the main teaching forms in turn, considering their purpose and exploring how to approach each one to get the most out of it.

At the start of your course you are probably full of enthusiasm; great! Make it last as long as you can, but recognize that there are certain ways to approach, for example, lectures or seminars which will help ensure you gain the intended results from them.

## Lectures

### The nature of lectures

Lectures are a characteristic feature of all undergraduate degrees. If you have come to university straight from school, the lecture is what will feel most different. The number of students in lectures will vary depending on the course, but in some cases may be in the hundreds. This is very different from learning in the school classroom. Typically there will not be the opportunity to ask questions or for clarifications during the lecture, rather you will listen to an academic speak on a topic, usually for just under an hour (possibly with time for questions at the end). Often the lecturer will be an expert on the topic they are presenting. This then is an excellent opportunity to learn key information and arguments. Used well, lectures can be a great short cut for you.

Sounds great, doesn't it? However, getting the most out of lectures is not always easy. Listening to someone talk for an hour can be tiring. Lecturers do not all have great presentation skills, and if you have a world-leading expert who mumbles, or a professor who just speaks off the cuff for an hour with no apparent structure, it can be hard to grasp their argument. So it's important to understand what lectures are designed to do; however well or badly they are delivered, the information presented will be critically important to developing your studies.

## The purpose of lectures

The best lectures will be well structured, full of interesting, relevant information and contain plenty of references for your private study. This is a key purpose of lectures on which you must be clear. They are a starting point, or way into a topic. They will not provide everything that you need to know about it. They should pave the way for interesting discussion in seminars, by presenting a range of arguments and views, so that you can start to develop your own critical thinking. Over a whole course the lectures will provide you with an overview of all of the key topics, and therefore can be useful when it comes to selecting essay questions later.

### Action

However much of a chore it may seem sometimes, always attend lectures (they are after all a small part of your total time). You cannot wind the clock back and once you have missed one, or more, you have removed something that could help from the route to good results.

## How to get the most out of lectures

It may be stating the obvious, but lectures demand a great deal of concentration. If you 'switch off' for any length of time you will have lost the thread of the argument. Focus your mind immediately prior to the lecture, and try to position yourself in the lecture hall so that you are not distracted by late arrivals, noisy heaters or fans, or students who tend to whisper as the lecturer talks. Make sure that you have everything you need to hand; the value of the lecture will drop significantly if your pen runs out of ink halfway through.

Note taking in lectures is essential. When it comes to writing an essay, or preparing for an exam, you will not be able to remember the detail of what has been said when you have several lectures every week. It is not possible to write down everything that is said. For a start you won't be able to keep up, and secondly you will lose the flow and structure of the lecture if you are constantly writing notes. You need to strike a balance, and experience will make this easier. Your notes should include:

- main and subheadings;
- key themes, questions or arguments;
- references and/or quotations;
- formulae and/or technical data;
- anything that you find particularly interesting (something that stimulates your curiosity is a great way back into a topic at a later stage when completing coursework).

Your notes are now a key study tool, so make sure they are written in a way that assists your future learning:

- Start your notes with details of the course, lecture title, lecturer and date. This will assist filing, and following up any points later. Ideally include a summary of this information on each page and make sure pages are numbered; when preparing coursework or revising you may have these notes out on your desk with a number of others and need to be able to put them away again in order.
- Write on only one side of the paper. When planning an essay it may be useful to have all your notes on a topic spread out in front of you.
- Leave plenty of space in your notes, for example use wide margins, to allow you to annotate them with additional information later in the lecture, or in future.

You will obviously need to write your notes as the lecture progresses, and so they will inevitably follow the structure of the lecture. However, it is worth thinking of keeping a lecture summary sheet in addition, to note key issues, references, and points for you to follow up. Such a summary sheet will inevitably vary by subject, but a suggested template that you may be able to adapt is given on the next page.

**TABLE 2.1**  Lecture summary table

| Course title | |
|---|---|
| Lecture title | |
| Lecturer | Date |
| Major themes<br>1.<br>2.<br>3. | |
| Important facts<br>1.<br>2.<br>3. | |
| Important figures, statistics or formulae<br>1.<br>2.<br>3. | |
| Important people and dates<br>1.<br>2.<br>3. | |
| Key references<br>1.<br>2.<br>3. | |
| Issues to follow up/ questions arising<br>1.<br>2.<br>3. | |

Given how important they are, you need to check that your notes, written in haste, are fit for purpose. After the lecture you need to find a short while to review them while the lecture is fresh in your mind, adding any detail that you think will be useful, and making sure they will be easy to understand at a later stage. You can also complete your summary sheet at this stage.

## Handouts and supporting information for lectures

Often lecturers will provide some kind of handout, for example a summary of the lecture, a copy of their slides or a list of references. During the lecture, annotate and highlight these. There is no need to duplicate notes already on the handout, but do not let these be a substitute for your own notes. Taking notes yourself not only provides a record of the lecture but is proven by a variety of psychological studies to help your understanding and memory (the physical and mental act of writing things down literally improves retention). These notes will be important when it comes to preparing coursework and revising for examinations.

In addition to any handout, there may be supporting information made available by the lecturer on the web. If this is available beforehand, try to read it in advance as it will certainly help you better understand the volume of material delivered in the lecture and put it in context. Never, under any circumstances, use such material as a substitute for attendance at the lecture. It is supporting, not replacement, material.

## Asking questions

Some lecturers allow time for questions at the end of a lecture, though not all do so and numbers attending can limit the number of questions that can be asked. This is an opportunity to quickly:

- clarify anything that was unclear during the lecture;
- follow up any points that were touched on only briefly, or other points of interest;
- ask the lecturer for their own view on the topic. Which of the arguments or angles do they agree with?

It is not, however, the time for in-depth debate on the topic. On most courses, you will have a seminar following the lecture which will allow for more detailed discussion with your fellow students and seminar leader, and it is to seminars that we now turn.

 Action

Always ask a question if necessary; checking afterwards can take longer and may give a less accurate answer.

# Seminars

## The nature of seminars

Seminars are the bread and butter of university courses. Typically they will involve a seminar leader (who may be a member of academic staff or a student studying for a higher degree) and, depending on your institution and course, about 15 students. This purpose of such seminars is to provide a forum for you to:

- check you have understood the arguments;
- contextualize information within each theme more widely;
- start to form your own viewpoints. Critical thinking is a key skill here (more of this later and in Chapter 4 particularly).

## How to get the most out of seminars

Seminars will require more preparation than lectures. Prior to the seminar you should:

- Make sure that you have attended, and review the notes of, any relevant lecture.
- Ensure that you have completed the appropriate background reading. This may be in a course reader, or you may need to consult books and articles listed in the bibliography.
- Make a list of, and/or brief notes on, any topics that you want to raise.

In a small group you are more exposed if you are not prepared. The work you do at this stage will also help you in identifying the topics that you wish to study further, perhaps for an essay or other piece of coursework.

Note taking in seminars can be more complicated than in lectures. Although the volume of material covered may not be as large as in a lecture, the discussion can be wide ranging and will certainly be less structured than in a lecture (or a good one, at least). You may not need to record every point in great detail if you are sure that you are not continuing study of this topic in future coursework. You need to take some notes, but may want to focus on things that help you synthesize the themes of the course effectively. Some notes will also certainly help you when it comes to revision time.

## Contributing to seminar discussion

You will get the most out of seminars only if you actively participate in them. Seminar leaders will try to encourage everyone to contribute, but university is not 'seventh form' and you will not be put on the spot in quite the same way as at school. It is up to you to calm any nerves and put your ideas forward. Don't think you will be invisible if you do not speak. Quiet students quickly stand out to seminar leaders.

The thought of speaking in a small group, when everyone is watching and listening, can make many students anxious. The first few contributions that you make in a seminar group may demand a lot of courage. This is especially true if the topic is new, and you do not feel confident of your facts. You might be worried that the point you want to raise seems obvious or is not relevant. One or two very confident students in the group who appear to be widely read and dominate the floor may make your nerves worse. However, rest assured that the majority of the group will feel the same as you. It is likely that if the topic is new to you it is new to them as well.

You need to overcome your nerves; the whole purpose of the seminar is to give you the opportunity to:

- develop and test your ideas;
- contextualize the material and arguments in this theme within the wider objectives of the course;
- ask questions and gain clarification from the seminar leader.

If you are confused about something, the chances are that several other people are too. It is therefore critical that you find an opening and volunteer your thoughts. Once you've done it a few times it will become much more natural, and in turn will encourage other students to chip in. A seminar is only as valuable as the group is prepared to make it. Don't rely on the seminar leader to deliver another lecture. You will miss out on the different learning and skills you can gain from an interactive seminar.

---

## Top tips...

### ...for overcoming nerves and speaking in a seminar

1 You don't need to make a long contribution. Make your point and then stop. The student who says the same thing in three or four different ways before they stop simply enjoys the sound of their own voice.

2 Think of a point or two to raise before the seminar, and make some brief notes to refer to.

3 Make sure you introduce your points at an appropriate time.

4 Look up and speak clearly. Don't mumble into your notes, however nervous you are.

5 Don't rush your contribution. Take your time, and if you feel your nerves taking over, pause, breathe deeply, and continue.

6 Check that your contribution has been understood (you can do this by asking, or looking at the signs on people's faces), and clarify if necessary.

7 Act confident, and you will start to feel it.

8 Make eye contact with those listening.

At some point in the course you may well be asked to give a presentation to your seminar group. Typically this is used by seminar leaders as a way of introducing each topic, with a different student kick-starting discussion with a brief presentation each week. This is covered in more detail in Chapter 7, but suffice to say at this point that if you are not used to speaking in seminars you may well find giving a presentation, which may be an assessed course requirement, extremely difficult; it is well worth some prior consideration.

## Listening to seminar discussion

Effective communication between the members of the group requires you to listen well, as well as make your own contributions. A good seminar will have the group exploring the detail of an argument through their banter. If your contribution changes the subject at a critical point because you have not been listening properly, the momentum of the discussion is lost.

---

**Top tips...**

**...for listening**

Effective listening is a skill. These points can help you become a better listener:

1  Look at the person speaking.

2  Focus on what they actually say; don't make assumptions. And don't jump to conclusions before they have finished speaking.

3  Clarify anything you don't understand (usually in a more informal seminar group this can be done immediately).

4  Think of questions that you can ask when they finish.

5  Contextualize their point within the wider theme of the week's seminar, and the course.

6  Concentrate; and take notes where appropriate.

7  Don't interrupt or speak to your neighbour.

---

Seminars are an excellent opportunity to advance your learning and hone your critical thinking skills. In addition, the strong group rapport that can be built up can act as a real motivator to study. Make sure that you make the most of this forum.

Action

Seminars are a vital part of your course. Get the best from them:
prepare for them, listen, participate and integrate what they give you
into your total learning experience.

# Practical classes

## The nature of practical classes

While lectures and seminars make up the vast majority of university classes,
there are other forms. If you are studying such fields as the creative arts, science
or medicine, your course is almost certain to involve practical sessions as
well. These may be in a computer or science laboratory, in a theatre or other
performance space, in an art studio, or in a hospital or other clinical setting,
but the key thing is that you are engaged in actually carrying out the activity
that you are studying.

Practicals give you the opportunity to put the theory you are learning in
lectures and seminars into practice. It is one thing to study a particular experiment, for example from books or in the lecture hall, but quite another to
attempt to recreate it in the laboratory (where mistakes can create a cloud of
smoke!).

## Laboratory practicals

Practicals in labs are typically 2–3 hours in duration (although they may get
longer in your final year) and occur once or twice a week. The cohort of students on the course will be broken down into smaller groups, to work through
a series of exercises, usually with support from the lecturer and either lab
technicians or PhD students. Practicals are not group work (although there
may be practical group projects as well at some stage in the course).
Sometimes students are simply brought together because of the facilities
needed to undertake the work. The exercises you work through are done
alone. The worksheets or lab books will be part of your assessment, and may
lead to a more substantial piece of written work such as a report or essay, or
may stand alone.

Such practicals are designed to extend your knowledge and skills and to
assess:

- that you know how to use the equipment correctly;
- your practical understanding of the theory;
- your thought process and workings;

- how you react when things go wrong (so learn what to do about that smoke);
- how you record the different stages of the practical work, and how you present the results.

All of these skills are ones that will develop as you undertake practical work; you are not expected to be an expert at the beginning of the course. Practical sessions also allow competent students to show real flair and individuality by going above and beyond the requirements. They are not testing that you get exactly the same results as you would get in a state-of-the-art research laboratory; the chances are that the equipment you are using is not sophisticated enough for this. So don't worry if you cannot replicate the result in the textbooks.

## *Other practicals*

But not all practical work is laboratory based. In the creative arts practical sessions may be much longer: a whole day, or a series of days on a particular assignment. In the performing arts you will usually be working in a group (of which more anon) with all the complexity entailed by that. Different students will be involved with different aspects of the production, including performing, stage management and direction. It is quite different from being in a laboratory where everyone is working through the same set of exercises. In the fine arts you are likely to be working alone, but possibly with other students around.

In all cases the purpose of the practical sessions is to develop a set of skills that you need to master to pass your course and cannot be taught only through theory. The end product of practical work (be it a completed lab book, a performance, or anything else) will therefore be part of your assessed work, and such sessions should always be taken as seriously as all other parts of your studies.

---

**Action**

Note that much practical work has a strong continuity involved: one thing leads to another and missing a session may, at worst, render the next session difficult or impossible to follow. So, make every effort to attend consistently.

---

# E-learning

The word e-learning is used increasingly in universities, and its meaning is often unclear or ambiguous. Put simply, e-learning is about using electronic resources to support your study. These resources fall into two main categories: 1) material and information which just happen to be in electronic form;

2) resources which provide an electronic learning platform. The first of these aspects is dealt with in the following chapter on information sources. Here we consider the second category of electronic learning platforms.

Most universities now use systems such as Moodle or Blackboard to support teaching. They are used in a variety of ways, including:

- Repositories of material such as course outlines, bibliographies, guidance on assignments and lecture notes (which means that they are always available on demand).

- The portal for the submission of assignments. BEWARE: this facility is nearly always linked to comprehensive plagiarism-detecting software and so acts as another deterrent to the temptation to plagiarize. See Chapter 6 for more information.

- Teaching tools in their own right. You could be asked to contribute to an online discussion, or make a statement on an e-notice board, or complete short tests or questionnaires.

- Hosting resources designed to assist you measure your own progress, such as learning diaries, incremental CV generators or personal development portfolios.

If you are required to use any such system you should familiarize yourself with it early in your course.

# Group project work

Depending on your course you may have to undertake project work in a group. This can be for a variety of reasons, and might involve writing a report, making a presentation or giving a performance. Whatever its form, the principles of working in a group are the same. While the change from private study is more than likely to be welcome, group work can be a mixed blessing. On the positive side, working in a group provides the opportunity for:

- learning from other students; information, ideas and study techniques;
- learning about group dynamics, and how you function in a group (both good and bad);
- talking through and developing your own ideas, often in a way that demands some creativity;
- ensuring that you focus; the group will need to concentrate and to set deadlines, and if you miss them you are letting down the others;
- developing the important interpersonal skills that are likely to be essential in future employment.

On the downside:

- You have less control than on an assignment on which you work alone.
- There may be personality clashes within the group.

- If the group does not work together effectively, there is less chance of a successful outcome.
- There may be members of the group who see it as an opportunity to let others take the strain and do not contribute; conversely, there may be two or three members who dominate discussion and do not let quieter students contribute.
- You need to fit in group meetings alongside your timetabled classes and private study, and finding a convenient time for everything may not be easy.

Clearly, achieving good group dynamics is important to the success of the group. This depends on each member of the group taking responsibility for making it work. Group members are likely to have different approaches and attitudes to study as well as different personalities. You may not even like some of the people in your group. Yet you are going to have to work with them, and work with them effectively, if you are to get a good mark for the project.

---

**Top tips...**

**...for being a good group member**

1   Listen to others (as mentioned in the section on seminars).

2   Appreciate the contribution of others.

3   Volunteer your ideas, but do not dominate the discussion.

4   Meet deadlines, for preparation as well as written work.

5   Do not reject other people's ideas; if they are wrong on something factual, correct them gently.

6   Encourage all members of the group to participate; those who are quiet may have excellent ideas and strategies to contribute.

---

As well as thinking about how you can be a good group member, think about the characteristics of effective groups. They will usually have:

- clearly defined individual roles and responsibilities, including a project leader or chair;
- a shared vision and ownership of the project;
- a fair allocation of work;
- no passengers letting others do all the work;
- deadlines which are agreed and adhered to by all members;

- addressed any problems that have arisen during their work;
- productive meetings.

This last point is worth developing further, as often the last thing meetings are is productive. Too often they fail to address the important issues, and the group is not able to move the project forward any better afterwards. Try to stick to the project business first, and then socialize afterwards. Socializing together is a great way to help the group bond, but your meetings will be most effective if you focus on what needs to be done first. Each meeting needs:

- A time and date convenient to all.
- An agenda, set and circulated in advance, to which everyone in the group has an opportunity to add.
- A start and end time, with both respected by all members.
- A brief but formal record; agree someone to do this in advance.
  It could be the same person at every meeting or change each time.
  The record does not need to detail every aspect of the discussion, but it should certainly note any decisions or actions.
- A set of rules by which you all agree to abide. For example, only one person will speak at a time, everyone's contributions will be respected and considered, the agenda will be followed, the leader will be allowed to chair the meeting. Note: the leader has specific duties so it is worth some thought and discussion. Just taking an instant volunteer may seem easy for everyone else, but may not be best. The leader's role must be well exercised (see box) and chairing a meeting is a useful skill so do not be afraid to take this on.

## The leader's responsibilities in meetings

The list that follows illustrates the range and nature of the tasks involved. If it seems a little businesslike, then it is because a businesslike approach is necessary. It also shows clearly that there are skills involved, perhaps skills which must be studied, learned and practised. Whoever is leading the meeting must:

- Command the respect of those attending (and if they do not know them, then such respect must be won rapidly by the way they are seen to operate).

- Do their homework and come prepared (ie having read any relevant documents and taken any other action necessary to help them take charge. They should also encourage others to do the same, as good preparation makes for more considered and succinct contributions to the meeting).

- Be on time: ie in sufficient time to get things organized before the session commences.

- Start (and finish) the session on time.

- Ensure that any administrative matters are organized and will be taken care of appropriately (eg refreshments, taking minutes).

- Start on the right note and lead into the agenda.

- Introduce people if necessary (and certainly know who's who themselves – name cards can help everyone at some meetings).

- Set, and keep, the rules.

- Control the discussion, and do so in light of the various people who may be present: the talkative, the strident etc.

- Ask questions to clarify where necessary. It is important to query anything that seems unclear and to do so at once. This can save time and argument, whereas if the meeting runs on with something being misinterpreted then it will become a muddle and take longer to reach any conclusion.

- Allow everyone to have their say, and indeed encourage those reluctant to speak – the meeting will benefit from all views.

- Act to keep the discussion to the point and avoid digressions.

- Listen (as in LISTEN, if the Chair has missed things then the chances of the meeting proceeding smoothly are low and it may deteriorate into 'But you said...' arguments).

- Watch the clock, remind others to do the same and manage the timing and time pressure.

- Cope with any upsets, outbursts and emotion.

- Summarize as necessary on the way through the session to make sure that complexities do not get out of hand.

- Provide the final word, summarizing and bringing matters to a conclusion at the end. Similarly linking to any final administrative detail, such as setting the date for the next action or further meetings.

- See (afterwards) to any follow-up action. This may be especially important when there is a series of sessions: people promise something at one and turn up at the next having done little or nothing about it.

Do not be overwhelmed by this; some of what is necessary is only a touch on the tiller, as it were. That said, all this must be done with patience, goodwill, good humour and respect for both all those present (and maybe others) and for the purpose of the meeting.

Group work is certainly a challenge. But do it successfully and it will result in new skills that you could never have gained from working alone, and hopefully a highly graded piece of work as well.

# Examinations

Even the most confident student is daunted by the thought of examinations. An exam is the culmination of your module, course or year's work; a single opportunity to show what you have learnt, without collaboration, in a fixed time. It will also be a significant contributor to your final grade. It is not surprising, then, that exams make students nervous; this is par for the course (pardon the pun). The problem is when these nerves become unmanageable and so paralyze you from taking the action that will help you tackle the exam confidently and successfully.

Here we outline the preparation and action you need to make at each stage of the process, from revision to post-examination post-mortem, to ensure that you manage your nerves, do yourself justice and get the results you want.

First, it is perhaps worth outlining what your lecturers expect from exams, and also what they do not expect.

Exams are different from coursework, with different time constraints and different parameters; they are testing different skills. Exams are designed to test your ability to contextualize information and arguments. It is important to keep this aim in mind as you revise, as you should not be looking to reproduce coursework material in an exam.

For example, consider the differences between an essay written as part of your coursework and in an examination:

| Coursework | Examinations |
| --- | --- |
| Answers a specific question in great detail | Synthesizes main themes, with a much wider sweep, in a shorter length piece |
| Rounded, discursive manuscripts | Cuts to the heart of the question as quickly as possible |
| Follows all academic conventions | No need for full references or bibliographies |
| Researched and written over a long period | Instant responses based on sound revision and understanding developed through course |
| Polished and well crafted throughout | Minor grammatical and spelling errors likely to be forgiven |

## Revision for exams

The thought of starting revision can be so overwhelming that many students put it off again and again, especially when you have a large number of exams looming in a relatively short timescale. But begin by thinking about what you already know. The start of your exam preparation goes back to the start of the course. In every lecture, practical, seminar, project or essay you are gathering information, and learning skills that will help you in the exams.

It therefore stands to reason that revision will not help you succeed in exams if you have not made the effort earlier in the course. If you haven't completed seminar readings or practical sessions, or if you have submitted sub-standard essays that have not answered the question, then you do not have time to go back and familiarize yourself with this material now. Revision is a time for reviewing what you have already learnt from lecturers, course-work and private study.

---

**Action**

If you know that your prior work has gaps then you must start thinking about revision sooner; you may even need a pre-revision catch-up stage.

---

But assuming you have been diligent through the course, planning your revision effectively will help you do well. It is a slog, no doubt about it, but there are techniques that can help you make the whole process manageable.

## Revision timetable

Creating a revision timetable is the first step, especially if you have more than one exam to do. If you are just revising for a class test or a one-off exam, then a timetable might not be needed, but in the majority of cases you will have a number of exams to tackle. Making a timetable before you start any revision is essential. The timetable should:

- Note the time and duration of each exam. Plus allocate a bit of time afterwards to wind down; you won't feel like going straight on to revise for another paper.
- Allocate time for the revision of each main section. Go through course by course. Revision is much easier to tackle in manageable chunks. Don't just allocate several days for each course.

- Break this down into sections which will allow you to tick off what you have done as you go (something that makes you feel you are getting somewhere).
  - A 'sectional' approach also allows you to mix up different courses, or aspects of one course, to avoid monotony (see later for how to select what to revise).
- Include breaks. Revision is hard work; you need regular breaks to help structure your day. Exercise will help clear your mind. So too will meeting friends, and forgetting about the detail of revision for a while will help manage any stress. If you are working hard, breaks are well-deserved rewards which help keep up your motivation.
  - But don't get drawn into the kind of break that turns into a distraction for the rest of the day, wrecking your timetable. Some days will be busier than others, especially once the exams start and you are juggling actually doing these with revision for the ones that remain, but make sure you have adequate time away from your desk.

An example revision timetable is shown on the next page. The timetable assumes that you:

- Are revising for five exams (one on each of five courses A, B, C, D and E) which take place over a seven-day period, with about a month before this free from teaching to revise.
- Have had a break of at least a few days and ideally a week since the end of teaching. Starting a major revision programme when you are already tired is not sensible.
- Schedule three revision sessions per day (here simply called morning, afternoon and evening) and that you include different types of revision activity in each session (including looking at past papers, drafting essays, reviewing lecture notes and revising with friends, see below for more details).
- Include regular brief coffee/meal breaks and exercise during the days you are revising.
- Found Course B the hardest, and need to allocate more time to this revision.

**TABLE 2.2** Example revision timetable

| | Morning | Afternoon | Evening |
|---|---|---|---|
| Day 1 | Course A | Course B | |
| Day 2 | Course C | Course D | |
| Day 3 | Course E | **Afternoon off** | |
| Day 4 | Course B | Course B | |
| Day 5 | Course D | Course C | |
| Day 6 | **Day off** | **Day off** | |
| Day 7 | *Flexi time* | Course A | Course B |
| Day 8 | Course E | Course B | |
| Day 9 | Course C | Course D | |
| Day 10 | Course A | Course B | |
| Day 11 | **Morning off** | Course C | |
| Day 12 | Course E | Course D | Course B |
| Day 13 | **Day off** | **Day off** | |
| Day 14 | Course B | Course A | |
| Day 15 | Course C | Course E | |
| Day 16 | *Flexi time* | *Flexi time* | |
| Day 17 | Course A | Course A | Course A |
| Day 18 | Course B | Course B | Course B |
| Day 19 | **Day off** | **Day off** | |
| Day 20 | Course C | Course C | Course C |
| Day 21 | Course D | Course D | Course D |

**TABLE 2.2** *Continued*

|  | Morning | Afternoon | Evening |
|---|---|---|---|
| Day 22 | Course E | Course E | Course E |
| Day 23 | **Morning off** | Course B | Course D |
| Day 24 | Course A | Course C | Course E |
| Day 25 | Course B | Course D | Course A |
| Day 26 | **Day off** | **Day off** |  |
| Day 27 | Course C | Course B | *Flexi time* |
| Day 28 | *Flexi time* | Course A | Course D |
| Day 29 | Course A | Course B | Course B |
| Day 30 | **Morning off** | Final revision on Course A |  |
| Day 31 | EXAM A | **Afternoon off** | *Flexi time* |
| Day 32 | Final revision on Course B | EXAM B |  |
| Day 33 | **Morning off** | Course C | Course D |
| Day 34 | Final revision on Course D | Final revision on Course C |  |
| Day 35 | EXAM C | EXAM D |  |
| Day 36 | **Morning off** | Final revision on Course E |  |
| Day 37 | EXAM E |  | Time to celebrate! |

## Key things to note about the example timetable

1  There is no revision scheduled for the night before an exam. If you have revised effectively over the period this will be unnecessary and an early night will be much better for you.

2  There are regular days and half days off, especially at the beginning of the timetable. Revision is a very intense activity, with the stress of the examinations at the end of it on top. It is important that you pace yourself at the start of the process to avoid becoming overtired before the end.

3  Some sessions are allocated to 'flexi time'. This is an unscheduled revision period when you can use the time to look at aspects of your work that have been more complicated or time-consuming than anticipated and require more attention. Your timetable must remain flexible throughout and you should always be prepared to change revision sessions in light of your progression.

4  Each course is allocated time for revision in the morning, afternoon and evening. This ensures that each course gets some attention at your most productive time of day, whenever this is.

5  About halfway through the timetable there is a whole day allocated to each course. Many students find it useful to be able to really concentrate on each course for an extended period like this, and it will often highlight areas of neglect in your revision. This time also marks the start of the more intense period of revision, with most evening sessions now also used.

Your revision timetable is unlikely to look like your usual routine. If you have a part-time job or family responsibilities, then organizing your revision timetable in good time will help you make any additional arrangements necessary.

Once your timetable is done you are ready to begin the hard work of revision.

## Top tips...

### ...for successful revision

- Look at past papers. These will show you the nature of questions that come up, and the structure of the exam paper, which might help you plan how you will divide up your time during the exam.

Be wary of trying to predict this year's questions based on past papers; students who do this and tailor their revision accordingly can get a nasty shock.

- Decide what to revise. You won't have time to revise everything on a course, and this is why looking at past papers is essential. If you know you need to answer two questions out of five, then you may want to revise three or four topics. But remember these should be broad topics as an exam question is likely to require you to draw together different strands of information.

- Review your notes. (Ensuring that these are well organized throughout the course will save you time when it comes to revision.) Use a highlighter pen for key points, quotations and references. Use index cards to record the main headings for each topic, or write essay plans ensuring that you know sufficient information in each section.

- Make sure that you don't just re-read your notes. You need to rewrite the information first in an alternative way (to ensure that you can express the concept in an exam even if you can't recall the exact words), then also in an abbreviated way. Ideally speak it out loud (this is where revising with a friend can help; more of this in a moment). This is a much more effective way of remembering information than simply reading it.

- Don't try to learn things parrot fashion – other than important facts, formulae, quotations or the like. This is not an effective way to get a sweep of the course or topic that you will need in an examination. You will be able to retain less information this way, and if you spend all your time learning one or two topics off by heart which then don't come up in the exam you are stuck.

- Revise with like-minded friends. Fixing a time to meet up, alongside private revision, can help you stick to your timetable and increase motivation, when you are getting bogged down. Swap essays with fellow students to help you learn about topics you haven't covered in detail.

- Practise writing timed essays. This isn't a skill you need for coursework, and practising before the exams will help you feel more confident during them. Don't look at your notes; this will only slow you down, and doing it from memory will show you where there are gaps in your knowledge.

- Try to devise your own compare-and-contrast practice questions. This will help you think about issues and arguments more broadly than in strict topic lines.

> ### Action
>
> If you become overwhelmed, don't give up or plough on relentlessly, taking nothing in. Stop, take a short break and relax, and then go back to your desk with a calm mind.

As well as taking breaks it is important to make sure that you get enough sleep when revising and sitting exams. This is a very intense period of study and can be draining. Sticking to your timetable will mean that you do not need to revise long into the night just to cover the core topics.

> ### Action
>
> You may want to personalize the list just itemized, certainly have a clear note of how you will proceed and make sure that you go about it on a systematic basis that fits the time available and allocated in your timetable.

## Just before the exam

The night before the exam try to get a good night's sleep. This is not the time for a big night out (even if you feel you need to forget what is to come the next day). Nor should you revise long into the night. If you start to get tired you will not be able to retain information, and are then likely to panic. At this stage, if you are well prepared, a good night's sleep is much more important. If you find it hard to drop off, don't panic. Don't lie in bed mentally going through revision notes if this keeps you awake.

Make sure you know how you are going to divide up your time in the exam. This will depend on how the marks will be allocated (looking at past papers should make this clear, but do check with your lecturers in case of any changes in format). It is all too tempting to spend the majority of your time on a topic you know well, but you need to spend it where the majority of marks are. You may want to adjust the provisional timings you propose in light of the questions when you see the paper, but it is no good spending an hour on the first answer if you have just two hours to answer three questions (assuming they carry equal marks).

**Practical tips...**

...for the morning of the exam

1   Take a last look through your index cards if you have time.

2   Avoid students who will undermine your confidence or who are stressed.

3   Don't worry about some nerves; these will actually help you focus in the exam (really!).

4   Eat sufficient food, even if your tummy is full of butterflies. You don't want to be distracted by hunger or embarrassed by a rumbling stomach.

5   Gather together the materials you need to take into the hall: pens (always take a couple of spares), water, your ID or any documentation you need, a warm fleece (exam halls are usually large and cold).

If you have followed the advice in this section you will be well prepared to tackle the exam and should be confident in your ability to do yourself justice.

## During the exam: 10 steps to exam success

### Step 1

Before you turn over the paper, make sure you are calm. Some deep breaths at this stage may help. Think too of all the revision you have done, and try to stay confident and focused.

Note: Read the paper through completely and make sure you understand it. Take very great care here; it may be obvious, but the world is full of students who have realized too late that they have not answered the question as they should have done.

### Step 2

If you have a choice of which questions to answer, don't rush to select them. A little longer spent at this stage, thinking about the structure and broad content required to answer, will ensure you make the right selection, and don't get half-way through an answer only to discover you don't have quite the right material at your fingertips. In particular, be wary of a question which sounds like something you have revised but has a different angle; don't go off down the wrong track.

### Step 3

Don't panic. If the questions don't reflect what you have revised, take a deep breath and review. Could you use parts of two or three topics you have covered to answer a question, for example?

## Step 4

If you feel you could tackle more than the number of questions required, then think carefully about which ones will allow you to best show the knowledge and views that you have.

## Step 5

If a question is in more than one part, make sure that you can answer each part; don't be drawn in by a question of which you can answer only one aspect.

## Step 6

Decide how long you will spend on each answer, and stick to it. Don't forget to check the clock every now and again. Remember to spend time according to the allocation of marks. If you run out of time on one of the questions, take two or three minutes only to jot down the rest of what you would have written in bullet points. Leave a suitable space before moving on to the next question. If you have time at the end you can return to the space you have left and complete your answer in more detail. Always remember to do your bullet point list before you move on to the next question, while the first topic is still foremost in your mind.

## Step 7

Make sure that you tackle each answer individually. You may wish to note down initial ideas for each question, but once you have started writing, focus on that particular question, and do so without distraction.

## Step 8

Plan and structure your answer before you start to write. It is not like using a computer where you can write the text in any order and go back to add large sections of text at a later stage. Time taken planning your answer is time well spent. Consider the number of scripts your examiner will have to mark. Make it easy for them to give you high marks by structuring your answer well, so the key points stand out. Don't forget that if you are writing an essay you will always need a clear structure: an introduction, conclusion and so on.

## Step 9

Once you have finished, take time to re-read your answers (you will need to allow for this in allocating time). You will be writing under pressure and at speed, and may need to tweak a few sentences to ensure their clarity. However brilliant the concept you are trying to express might be, it will not gain you any marks if your lecturer cannot understand what you mean. Similarly, as we are all so used to using computers these days our handwriting is sometimes not what it might be, especially when writing at length. You must ensure that your responses are legible, and appropriately laid out for formulae, mathematical symbols and the like.

## Step 10

It is unlikely that you will be able to leave the examination hall before the end of the exam. If you finish significantly early, check if you have completed the paper correctly and answered the right number of questions. If you do have some time then don't waste it, use it to check your answers again. Correcting spelling and grammar will improve clarity; any aspect of your work you find to positively amend may usefully improve it further.

However worried they were before the exam, most students are surprised at how time flies by. Exams demand the kind of intense focus that is not required for other forms of assessment, and before you know it you'll hear the words 'time's up'.

## *After the exam*

The relief that you feel at the end of an exam, however you think you may have done, is very real. It is inevitable that you will want to discuss the paper with friends, discuss which subjects came up, which questions you answered and so on. However, be wary of discussing your answers in too much detail with others. It is too late to change anything now, and you don't want to be reminded of points you may have forgotten, or worry about whether you should have tackled a particular question in another way. This will only make you nervous for the next exam that you face.

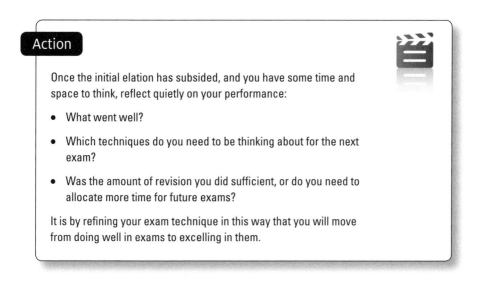

### Action

Once the initial elation has subsided, and you have some time and space to think, reflect quietly on your performance:

- What went well?

- Which techniques do you need to be thinking about for the next exam?

- Was the amount of revision you did sufficient, or do you need to allocate more time for future exams?

It is by refining your exam technique in this way that you will move from doing well in exams to excelling in them.

**Read on...**

In this chapter we've looked at the major types of teaching methods you'll encounter on your course, as well as the examinations that test your knowledge and understanding at the end of it. But of course much, if not most, of your study will be outside of these formal settings, in libraries, on computers and at your desk. So it is to the vitally important issue of information gathering and absorption that we turn in the next chapter.

## Your notes

...................................................................................................................

...................................................................................................................

...................................................................................................................

...................................................................................................................

...................................................................................................................

...................................................................................................................

...................................................................................................................

...................................................................................................................

...................................................................................................................

...................................................................................................................

...................................................................................................................

...................................................................................................................

...................................................................................................................

...................................................................................................................

...................................................................................................................

...................................................................................................................

...................................................................................................................

...................................................................................................................

...................................................................................................................

# 03
# Information gathering and absorption

**In this chapter...**

We turn now to **sources of information**: course materials, the university library, electronic resources and others. The information you learn from lectures and seminars is only a starting point – everything else you need you'll have to gather yourself. To do this you will also need to understand and assess the quality of the information sources, and know what is not appropriate for university-level study as well as what is. Fortunately, no one will expect you to be an expert in your subject at the start of your course. As Samuel Johnson said, 'Knowledge is of two kinds. We know a subject ourselves, or we know where we can find information upon it.'

## Learning for yourself

As an undergraduate you will undertake far more extensive research into subjects than at any previous stage of your education. One of the exciting challenges of a degree programme is the extent to which you learn through your own exploration as you pursue information and put pieces together, large and small, to inform your studies.

Lectures and seminars are only a framework for your studies, and do not provide all the material that you will need for your course. It is your task to build upon these through independent study. This is a fundamental point and it is critical that you grasp it right at the start of your studies.

## The volume of material available

Universities are vast repositories of information and knowledge, and you will become an expert in navigating your way through those collections during your course. The process of navigation will often bring you into contact with sources you either had no idea existed in the first place, or, if aware of them, never thought you'd be able to access easily and use. (This is particularly true of specialist primary source collections held by some university libraries.) Given the volume of information available, gathering the right information for a particular course, seminar, essay or assignment is an interesting challenge. There are various ways of going about it, with the university library usually acting as the hub.

---

### Definition

#### Primary and secondary sources

Primary sources are the original materials upon which all interpretations and subsequent studies are based.

Secondary sources are the subsequent studies and interpretations by academics and others over the following years (sometimes many hundreds of years; it is not a primary source just because it is old).

Sources are many and varied and link appropriately to your chosen subject. For example, for an English Literature student primary sources will include novels, poetry and other literature. For a History student they will include diaries, letters and government papers.

---

## The right material

It is critically important that you access the right type of information for your private study. You need material that is sufficiently comprehensive in terms of its depth of analysis and range of conclusions. This means that recycling material or sources from previous study, for example A levels, is usually inappropriate, and should never be done without checking with lecturers first. Material on the world wide web should also be used with caution, and this is covered in more detail below. Fortunately, guidance on sources of information will be provided by lecturers in the form of a bibliography.

## *Bibliographies*

Outside of your lectures and seminars, the first stop for information is the course outlines (a summary of topics to be covered) and bibliography.

A bibliography is a list of books and other relevant reference material (including primary and secondary sources) relating to a particular course. It is usually structured by topic. Where the bibliography is extensive you would not be expected to read everything listed, although you may need to consider all material in a particular topic if you are preparing a seminar presentation or essay.

Lecturers spend a great deal of time preparing course outlines and bibliographies, revising them regularly and taking care to ensure a spread of material designed to give you an overview of the various opinions and interpretations of each topic you study. This material is invariably held by the university library, or if not, the lecturer will identify an easily accessible alternative source.

## *Core texts*

Many courses have core texts associated with them which will be flagged in the bibliography. It may be worth investing in at least one of them, and you may need to consult them so frequently that repeated borrowing from the library is not really practical and just wastes your time. But before you buy, do have a look at a library copy. There is no point spending money on a text that you will not use. Instead, discuss it with your lecturer and survey the core texts before investing in a selection of them. The second-hand book market is very helpful for saving money, and if you're lucky, a ton of valuable marginal notes! Your university may have a second-hand bookshop, or a number of internet book sites are now available.

Note: If you think you have found something of relevance to your module, but it is not on your bibliography, it is worth checking it with your lecturer. It may be that you have made a genuine discovery, or it might be something your lecturer has deliberately omitted because it is not regarded as suitable for university-level study.

**Action**

The bibliography is the most important piece of information you need for each course. It is a signpost to the different sources you will need to study to do well. Make sure you follow its guidance.

## *Module readers*

Lecturers often produce module readers which are a photocopy of all the core material relating to each week's subject on a course. This will save you time hunting down the most essential material in the library. As with bibliographies, readers are produced with a good deal of care and so form vital initial insights into a subject. To get the best out of module readers:

- Do not consider them as the last word on the subject, but a useful introduction.
- Read the relevant sections as a minimum before each lecture and seminar.

Owing to photocopying and reproduction costs, departments usually ask students to buy reader packs, but the sum is invariably far cheaper than photo-copying the material yourself or using printer credits (see below) to print out downloaded pieces. As well as providing hard copy, lecturers often put this material on intranet sites. This is particularly useful if you happen to mislay any of your module materials as its 24-hour access means you need never be without them for long.

# The university library

The university library will become a second home to most students during the course of studying for their degree. University libraries are usually very impressive in terms of the sheer amount and range of material that can be found in them. They are usually much bigger physically and in terms of their collections than any school, college or municipal library you've ever visited or used, and for that reason can seem rather daunting on first contact. In order to demystify the library most universities run induction sessions for first year students. These are usually arranged by degree or subject to ensure that you get the right kind of specialist briefing and advice.

### Action

Promptly after arrival at university, make every effort to get to your library induction meeting. (Fortunately, there is often more than one meeting for each cohort of students and so if for some reason you cannot make your allocated session, do make sure that you sign on for an alternative time.) If you do not do this you risk putting yourself at a real disadvantage.

## Catalogues

The catalogue(s) is the central database of all library material which provides full bibliographic detail as well as how to find each item. As mentioned earlier, universities are vast repositories of information in which the library dominates. Therefore alongside the traditional resources of books there will be:

- academic journals (see below for more information);
- DVDs;
- videos and CD-ROMs;
- slide and photograph collections;
- newspapers (both recent and archived);
- collections of MA, MPhil and PhD theses by the university's postgraduates;
- electronic access to a huge range of digital collections; and more.

Understanding the catalogues, and this almost invariably means the e-catalogue, and the classification system (which relates to the location of each discipline and their subdivisions) is crucial to locating and using information success-fully. The induction sessions will help, and it is worthwhile backing those up by sitting down and taking time to play with the catalogue. This will help you to find out all the specific elements of your institution's system. On first use you will find that most cataloguing systems are designed to reveal every possible item relating to your query. It is therefore important to know how to narrow your search. This is done most effectively by knowing how to limit searches by subcategory, including:

- specific title;
- author name;
- type of material (for example book, journal article or DVD).

## Borrowing rights

Another vital thing to understand is for how long you can borrow any item. University libraries often ring-fence the most important – or scarce – material for particular modules in what are called core-text or short loan collections. This means that a certain book or other material is available for only a relatively short space of time; sometimes it can be for as little as three hours. In other cases it is 24 hours or a week. (This means that planning and time manage-ment are critical skills you need to develop, see Chapter 1.) Other material is usually available on longer loan, often for between a fortnight and three weeks.

If you find that a library item of particular interest to you is unavailable, do not be afraid to put in a recall request. The library will then contact the person currently issued with the book and ask them to return it immediately. Do not be afraid to use this service. It can be particularly important if a lecturer or other member of academic staff has the item as their borrowing rights are often for far longer periods – up to a year in some cases – and so waiting for it to come back to the library is not an option.

---

### Action

Always ensure that material you borrow from the library is returned by the specified recall date and time and that you handle and store the materials carefully.

Handing back material after the deadline, or the losing or damaging of items (even if entirely accidental), usually results in penalties, often the suspension of borrowing and other library rights, which can have serious implications for your study. One of the biggest gripes students have about their fellows is the late return of books or the return of damaged items which means that their withdrawal for repair or replacement makes them unavailable at least for a while.

---

## Subject librarians

Nearly all university libraries have staff who specialize in certain parts of the collection. Good subject librarians can be invaluable allies who will help you master the catalogues and thus the seemingly endless shelves and e/virtual collections.

For those working in the humanities and some arts subjects, the reliance on books and journal articles is still overwhelming and is driven by the long-established practice of reading continually and extensively. For example, those working in the sciences and certain sections of the social sciences may find that their reading is more tightly focused, but it will still be through the library as a physical or virtual entity that provides it.

## Using other libraries and inter-library loans

Occasionally, you might need specialist material unavailable in your university library. This occurs most often in courses which require larger-scale, in-depth pieces of work such as dissertations. Your university library can usually help to track a particular item down. Many university libraries have agreements with each other allowing students access, although usually not lending rights, to each other's collections (meaning you would need to go and visit the other library to see the item).

In addition, your university library can carry out an inter-library loans search. These often require the consent of your lecturer in the form of a signature on a request slip, but this should not cause any difficulty. In this case the book will be sent to your library from the holding library and you will be notified when it arrives. But this will take time, and thus again highlights the importance of planning your study, and coursework in particular, to flag such requirements in advance.

## Academic journals

A resource often novel to new students is that of the journal article. A journal is like a magazine. It is published regularly and contains scholarly articles (sometimes around a specific theme), book reviews and sometimes other material. The articles are submitted by academics based on their current research and are all peer-reviewed. This means that before they are accepted for publication they are examined anonymously by other academics in the field for intellectual quality and rigour. All academic disciplines have a range of specialist journals attached to them which are usually a mixture of the general and specific.

For example, *Nature* is a famous journal which carries articles on any aspect of science. At the other end of the scale, but still within the group of academic scientific journals, is *Nature Nanotechnology*, which is obviously a highly specialist area. The humanities have their equivalents. For instance, *History* is a general journal publishing articles on a wide range of historical subjects, whereas the *Journal of Military History* is, as its title suggests, much more tightly focused.

Academics find articles particularly useful because they:

- contain the latest thinking on a subject;
- analyse specific themes or ideas within a wider context;
- provide succinct explorations of much broader topics.

---

**Action**

Journal articles are the stock cubes of the academic community – they contain concentrated learning. It is for this reason that many course bibliographies will contain large numbers of journal articles. Do not overlook these; they can provide useful information.

---

Those studying the sciences will get used to this form of information. The pace of change in scientific research often demands that information is released quickly and so science students can spend a lot of time reading relatively short pieces. Among arts and humanities undergraduates there can be a reluctance to engage with the journal literature. This is often because these types of undergraduates regard anything short of a weighty tome as lacking authority and insight. This feeling sometimes betrays a lack of confidence in the basic material, with the student thinking 'how can I tackle something on a specific element within this topic when I don't think that I understand the wider background?'. This is where you must use articles in conjunction with other, perhaps more wide-sweeping material, such as books.

It is also worth remembering throughout your course that lecturers would not put journal articles on the reading list if they were not highly relevant to your studies.

# Electronic resources

These are the other half of the e-learning resources mentioned in the last chapter.

## *Electronic journals*

Journal articles are also very handy for another reason – increasing numbers of academic journals are available electronically and therefore, unlike books, unlimited numbers of students can access them at the same time. (Indeed, some journals are published only in electronic form.) What is useful clearly varies enormously depending on the subject being studied, but most universities provide guidance (ask if it seems more is needed) and in some cases provide passwords to access recommended sites.

All university libraries subscribe to a range of academic journal host services and their websites usually provide a portal through which to access them. In some instances complete runs are available stretching back to the 19th-century origins of the oldest academic journals, but in others it might be only issues from the past 10 to 30 years. However, university libraries will usually have hard copies of anything unavailable electronically and these are usually on restricted loans and so, once again, access is not too difficult.

## *Books*

The digitizing of books is still relatively slow compared with that of journals, but there are a number available, and, like articles, your university library will subscribe to certain services which will be made clear on the library website. Any comment here will quickly date, but many sources will become relevant depending on your field of study, and it is something to check.

## *World wide web*

As well as many of the traditional hard-copy resources becoming available electronically, a host of other electronic and digital forms of information and material exists. The web has undoubtedly transformed the way we lead our lives and has been very helpful in education and academic research, but it can be a minefield and it is extremely important that you are aware of its pitfalls.

## The nature of web material

There are very, very few academic assignments which can be completed by use of the web alone; indeed, lecturers will take a dim view of students who use this tactic.

We are often told that the web is an extremely egalitarian and democratic form of communication, indeed anyone can post almost anything they like on it. However, that does not mean that everything on it is of equal quality and academic value. It. Is. Not. As you will know from your wider use of the web, it is a hotbed of rumour-mongering, gossip and, occasionally, downright pernicious lies. Lecturers therefore tend to list in their bibliographies only what they consider to be useful web resources. You will find that you won't get much in the way of praise and good marks if you base your research on uncritically Googling words. The crucial difference between unfettered and directed use of the web is the element of quality control and discrimination the latter provides.

As noted above, when academics publish journal articles they have to go through the vetting processes of having their work reviewed by other academics in their field. The same rules apply to publishing with reputable firms, and all university presses in particular. Therefore anything you read in an academic journal or university press book has benefited from many layers of critical input from a range of specialists. By contrast, taking all of your knowledge on International Law from, say, the self-proclaimed South-West Croydon International Law Focus Group (with a special interest in the Rice Krispies trade) website might not be that useful.

Certain websites have a surface academic respectability. One such is Wikipedia, but this is by no means a reputable source and is deeply susceptible to tweaking by those who just want to have a laugh or who do so for more malicious purposes. Therefore, when it comes to the web, it is vital to remember the glaring inequalities of status for academic purposes. Just as you would never write a theology essay by reference to the film *The Life of Brian* (that is, unless it specifically asked you to discuss the impact of film on theology!), the same is true for web resources.

---

### Action

Be discerning in your selection and use of materials. Stick to the bibliography and you won't go wrong. Avoid material which has no critical analysis or a narrow range of conclusions. If in any doubt contact your lecturers for advice.

## *Library portals*

Fortunately, your university library has often done the hard work for you. Working with lecturers, university library websites usually provide the portal for accessing the most valuable electronic academic resources. There is an excellent range of material freely available through most university libraries.

If, for example, you are a student of Politics and International Relations, you will find that your institution has access to all parliamentary papers. Historians can explore resources such as pre-20th century parliamentary papers and the British Library's digitized collection of 19th-century newspapers. Law students will find the latest collections of legal papers from judicial centres such as the European Court of Human Rights. These types of electronic resource can support your studies brilliantly and keep you away from the more weird and wonderful corners of the web.

Of course, once you have accessed these electronic resources you might well find that you need hard copy. University IT systems will usually allow you to download and print out material on payment of a small charge. This is often managed through internal debit cards which work by a system of credits on a pay-as-you-go basis. This system often covers a wide range of internal services, from use of the cafeterias to printers and photocopiers.

# Extracting the information you need

Once you have tracked down the book, article, or whatever you need, you need to identify the relevant information. In some cases this may be only a small amount on a few pages, in others a whole section, or possibly the whole text.

The best way to extract information is to determine exactly what it is that you need. Start this process by looking closely at the content pages, indices or abstracts (depending on the type of material). Use keywords to identify which pages or parts you need to read closely. Don't get drawn into parts of the author's argument or narrative which are not relevant to your purpose.

Once you've started this process you can contact your lecturer, explain the direction you are taking, and check that this is appropriate.

Making notes as you read is critical. You may wish to record:

- a summary of the argument or approach;
- any key quotations, facts or dates;
- questions and issues that need further study or discussion with lecturers.

Make sure that you always record the precise bibliographic details of your sources, so that you can refer back, or include them in coursework.

# Summary

The identification and absorption of information is something you do in a variety of ways and with much support from your lecturers and other members of university staff. However, it also requires your hard work and intelligent and careful assessment of some resources in order to ensure that you access material of the right quality.

**Read on...**

Gathering and absorbing the information that you need for your course, as discussed in this chapter, is not sufficient at university level. You will also need to contextualize it within a wider framework, and then to assess, analyse and interpret it. It is to these skills that we turn in the next chapter.

# Your notes

..................................................................................................
..................................................................................................
..................................................................................................
..................................................................................................
..................................................................................................
..................................................................................................
..................................................................................................
..................................................................................................
..................................................................................................
..................................................................................................
..................................................................................................
..................................................................................................
..................................................................................................
..................................................................................................
..................................................................................................

# 04
# Analysis

**In this chapter...**

As a university student you will need to **collect facts** – some degree programmes require you to collect and know thousands – but crucially, this is often only a tiny part of the process. The real skills you need to develop are selecting facts and information judiciously, and then assessing and interpreting it intelligently, to show that you command not only the raw material of your degree programme, but the ability to interconnect and interpret it, too. As Sherlock Holmes says, 'I ought to know by this time that when a fact appears opposed to a long train of deductions it invariably proves to be capable of bearing some other interpretation.'

## Starting with facts

The following statements are all facts:

1 The Battle of Hastings took place on 14 October 1066.
2 Charles Dickens wrote *Hard Times* in 1854.
3 There are more stars in the sky than grains of sand on the entire Earth.
4 3+1=4.
5 The River Hooghly reaches the sea at Calcutta.

While all of these facts are true, their significance and meaning can be debated. Facts gain meaning only when they are placed in an argument or used to illustrate a point, otherwise they are merely pieces of information.

Facts are the Lego bricks in your construction set. First, you must gather your bricks together. Chapter 3 pointed out ways of identifying, researching and collecting material. But, once you have gathered your Lego pieces together you will rapidly realize that as individual blocks they don't really have much significance.

# Using facts to construct something significant

This brings in the next stage – the ability to put them together in order to make something more interesting and significant. Most often this 'something' will be an argument or point of view you develop in written coursework or a seminar presentation.

At school and college you are usually given far more guidance on these two processes and they are made more focused still by the fact that the materials for study and the assignments set are also much narrower. At university you will be carrying out far more research by yourself, with lecturers providing advice, but not usually spoon-feeding you an entire plan.

To continue the Lego comparison, at university you move from Duplo to Lego Technic! This chapter is about finding good construction plans for your Lego bricks, which is a hugely important part of your degree programme.

# How to approach research

Initial research into a topic often brings in a vast haul of material and information and this can be daunting. The pleasing sensation of having a great stash of material can easily be offset by the fear of having to sort through it. This is why it is extremely important always to bear in mind the point of your study and the kind of material, information and facts you need. A good way of achieving this is to analyse the precise nature of your tasks:

- Exactly what have you been asked to do?
- If it is an essay question, precisely what does that question mean?
- If it is a laboratory practical, what kind of preliminary preparation and knowledge will assist you in its execution, enabling you to gain more from the experience?

Engaging with this process of questioning before you commence any detailed study is important as it gets your brain into gear and fires your critical faculties. As you start to consider precisely what you need to know and exactly how to go about the research, don't be afraid to ask your lecturers for their advice. After all, they are in their job because of their expertise and it is part of their role to inform and assist you in your tasks. They certainly won't do the work for you, but they will always provide help for the student who is actively engaged in their studies and assignments.

In researching material you should be involved in two parallel and inter-woven processes. You must:

1 continually ask yourself what sort of things you need to know in order to advance your studies or deal with a specific assignment;

2 treat everything you do find out as if it is animate and ask it a list of questions to help you get the best from it and interpret it effectively.

# Interrogating your facts

At university the basic facts of any subject or topic are simply taken as read by the lecturers. That you will seek out and acquire the facts is assumed. What they are really interested in and are testing you on is your ability to interpret these facts, thus implicitly giving them a value and ranking.

Getting meaning and value out of facts is done by questioning. Think of facts as real living people and ask them questions. Like the best crooks in crime series, once apprehended facts are prepared to sit things out in deafening silence. You must act like a good detective and interrogate your facts closely. The art of academic interrogation (ie analysis) lies in the ability to draw up a good list of questions to put before your facts.

# Using secondary sources to help your analysis

Fortunately, you are given a huge help in assessing and prioritizing the importance of facts in the core materials for your programme: the course bibliography will highlight a selection of the most important material.

The way students access facts is usually through the work of others and, of course, that means ploughing your way through the interpretations others have placed on those facts (the secondary sources – see definition in Chapter 3). Academics have spent millions of hours sorting through them and arguing over them for you.

## *The nature of secondary sources*

However, this means that everything on the reading lists for your modules contains the inbuilt value judgement of an academic. Academics don't produce 'pure' knowledge – if they did there never would be any debate or argument about anything – instead, they interpret and construct arguments based on their understandings of the sources and facts. This means that everything they write and say has been put together to persuade the reader to understand something in a certain way. It does not mean that they are engaged in some dreadful con trick, it is merely a reminder of what was said at the opening of this chapter: facts exist, but the meaning of them can be seen in different ways. Some things you read for your degree programme will have very subtle messages in them which can be difficult to detect, while others are blatant and easily perceptible. This is a critical point to grasp early in your studies.

Thus, when engaged in study with the aim of prioritizing, assessing and interpreting facts you must ask the following questions:

- Which facts does Professor X mention in the book/article?
- What interpretation and value does he/she place on them? And, critically,
- Is this the only/generally agreed way of looking at these facts?

To answer this final question, you will need to refer to other material. You don't want to discover that you have relied on one interpretation if there are others available. Don't be the person who relies upon the one piece arguing that the Earth's core is made out of Jaffa Cakes, as this might be a deliberately set academic trap to test whether you are researching widely enough and are assessing and interpreting with due care and discrimination.

Gaining the techniques to be able to determine the value of the Jaffa Cake theorist demands time and care. Only by allocating time to reading the materials supporting your lectures and seminars carefully and in close comparison with each other can your critical insight be sharpened. There are three techniques that may help you to do this.

## Assess the methodology

While reading or studying any collection of material, information, data or facts, a judgement as to their value can be gained by examining the methodology behind the material.

Note: methodology is a term referring to the processes used by academics to carry out their research and is applicable to all disciplines – sciences, social sciences, and arts and humanities.

Assessing the value of a methodology is a very good way into the issue of assessing the value of the overall interpretation of the facts. For instance, the value of a scientific article might be dependent upon the number and type of experiments carried out in order to gain the data and reach certain conclusions. If this is the case, the authors should be trying to prove their points by clear reference to this method.

To take an example from the humanities, an interpretation of a novel might require constant reference to the novel itself, and other writings and material by the novelist. If such references were missing, you might question whether the examination was rigorous enough. Assessing the value and rigour of a metho-dology, and through it the quality of the interpretation and conclusions, can also be assisted by close reference to the footnotes. Academic studies are usually footnoted in full. An important aspect of an academic's work is the open display of sources allowing others to check them if they wish; then, if they believe the interpretation misguided in some way, they can query and challenge it.

> ### Action
>
> Don't ignore footnotes. You can take any book or article and look carefully at the footnotes and sources which reveal much about both the breadth and depth of the original research. In addition, you might well be able to access the sources listed in their footnotes, check them out and consider whether you agree with the analysis or not.

## Read reviews and abstracts

With time often of the essence in so many aspects of university study, identifying the interpretations put upon facts can be greatly assisted by the careful reading of abstracts and reviews. Most academic journal articles are accompanied by what is called an 'abstract'. This is a précis of its content and of the overall argument presented and often appears on the opening page of an article. Reading the abstract carefully is not a substitute for reading the entire piece, but it highlights immediately and clearly the interpretations of the author(s) and gives you something to anchor your thoughts on as you progress through the piece.

Book reviews also often provide very good summaries of a work's content and add the second interesting element of revealing the opinions of the reviewer. Thus, a book review should not be taken as a definitive interpretation of a piece, but as one which might open up other questions and areas for you to consider. Such techniques are all about reading for, and identifying, an argument and interpretation which have been laid on top of the bare facts. They help you to establish the agenda academics have put on their fact selection.

## Identify the academic consensus

As we have already said, an important part of the process of analysis is determining the extent to which there is agreement over the meaning of facts and the degree to which there is dissent. Within this stage there are two elements to keep in mind. First, academics may agree generally on the broad outline of something, but disagree on precise details. Secondly, a discipline, or more likely subsections within it, might be far more confused with very little agreement on any interpretation and showing instead a broad series of differing interpretations. Once again, close reading is a good technique as academics, particularly in the introductory and concluding sections of their pieces, often position their work in relation to others'. In this way, you will be able to sketch out whether there are dominant interpretations and how deeply they are divided from minority positions. This process should prove a fascinating part of your studies and will serve to expand your intellectual vision greatly. It is also an integral part of the shift towards university-level study.

**Action**

Recognize that it is how you deal with facts that helps you make the most of them and adopt a systematic and thorough approach to how you work with them.

# Constructing an argument

A collection of facts and other information is merely raw material for the construction of an argument. We have established that nearly all the supporting materials you will use during your studies are interpretations and arguments built on facts. Accessing these works is also the first steps you take towards constructing your own arguments.

Your lecturers want to see your opinion and arguments come through in both written pieces and oral presentations, and it needs to be a considered and informed opinion. Your arguments only make sense and seem credible when they are grounded in fact and show an awareness of competing interpretations. A strong argument stands up because it arranges the facts logically and convincingly and reveals that it can overcome different assessments and conclusions. This means that an argument needs to be balanced; but that doesn't necessarily mean that it comes to no firm conclusion. Most academics take a good deal of time and trouble in their own research work to show that they are aware of other opinions, and then carefully point out where they think there is room for debate or an alternative explanation.

**Top tips...**

...for developing a credible argument

1 Do sufficient preliminary research to be confident of interpretations academics have made of the facts. (For those in the sciences, this might mean reference to relatively few and relatively short texts; for those in the arts and humanities, it may well involve reading which is both broader and deeper.)

2 Discuss your preliminary thoughts with your lecturers and let them know how your thinking on the topic is developing. This

can be very useful in refining your approach and minimizing any tendency to branch off in the wrong direction.

3  Look at the way academics have structured their arguments. Ask yourself:

   – how they have started the piece;

   – how they rank material in the main body;

   – how they conclude.

# Refining your argument

It is important to remember that all arguments and interpretations require refinement and are rarely perfectly formed the first time you either think them through or write them down. This is where discussion and interaction with others come into play. You can do this in two ways:

- The informal approach is to talk about your studies and specific topics within it with your fellow students. This may sound slightly nerdy, but it really helps. After all, your fellow students on a programme or module should all be enthusiastic about the basic subject material and so comparing thoughts on different topics may well open up other ways of thinking about a subject or refining your own interpretations further.

- The formal route is to maintain a dialogue with your lecturers and other students. There is, of course, a clear mechanism for just this kind of interaction: this involves seminars. Seminars are forums for discussion and the presentation of arguments. Use them as opportunities to debate interpretations of facts and gain the opinion of your lecturer and fellow students (see Chapter 2).

In addition to using seminars to refine your argument, think about how your lectures are presented. Your lecturers will usually deliver lots of facts and it sometimes might seem hard to keep up with that flow, but an important element to keep in mind is the interpretation the lecturer is placing upon the facts. How are they presenting those facts to you? Some lecturers might make it easier than others by being explicit. For example, they might state overtly something like this: 'My vision of this material is ABC, but if you read Professor QWERTY on this you will find that she says XYZ.' Others might be more subtle and the message is imbedded in the presentation. If you want to check that you have understood properly, then ask. Lecturers love it when their audience follows up on a point – it proves that people are listening!

# Using practicals to help

Outside of classes and lectures, you can also maintain contact with your lecturer on each step in the development of your interpretation of the facts of a topic. In supervised, practical work, for example a supervised experiment or drama improvisation, where a large group might be following a similar exercise, you have the perfect opportunity to ask questions about the methodology:

- Why are you all carrying out the same tasks in the same way?
- What does this show you about the basic material of your studies and who devised this particular way of approaching it?

However you do it, refining your argument before finalizing the coursework in which you present it for assessment is really important.

# Summary

These points are relevant across the spectrum of degree programmes – scientists change their interpretations of facts as readily as those working in the social sciences and humanities – and establishing knowledge of the schools of thought on various issues is an important part of many degree courses.

## Action

The student's job is not just to collect and store facts. What is needed is not just a passive process, but a creative one – you need to be an inspired interpreter of facts because it is that which makes them useful. You need to think carefully about how others have approached and interpreted things and form views and construct arguments that relate to the broad overall picture you find.

Mastering the art of interpretation and critical thinking will give you the immense satisfaction of knowing that you are not a pub quiz bore who can reel off facts merely because you have a photographic memory and no life, but that you have a fully rounded intellectual grip on your subject. It is also a priceless transferable skill. You will be able to tell any future employer that information collection, analysis and interpretation is one of your core competencies.

## Read on...

So far in this book we have discussed the kind of work that will be required of you at university, the skills you will need to do it, and the types of teaching methods you may encounter. All of these will be significantly different to what you have come across before. The level of independent analysis and work may seem daunting. Indeed, completing a university programme is a significant endeavour, and you will need support along the way. The range of support available is what we explore in the next chapter.

# Your notes

..........................................................................................................................

..........................................................................................................................

..........................................................................................................................

..........................................................................................................................

..........................................................................................................................

..........................................................................................................................

..........................................................................................................................

..........................................................................................................................

..........................................................................................................................

..........................................................................................................................

..........................................................................................................................

..........................................................................................................................

..........................................................................................................................

..........................................................................................................................

..........................................................................................................................

..........................................................................................................................

..........................................................................................................................

..........................................................................................................................

..........................................................................................................................

# 05
# Getting support from academic staff and others

**In this chapter...**

We consider now the **range of people** who can provide the help and support that you will need at university. Very few, if any, students can succeed in their course in complete isolation. Yes, university should be great fun, but it is also hard work, and will certainly be very pressurized at times. Looking for support from those around you is not just sensible, but necessary. As Jean de La Fontaine said, 'People must help one another; it is nature's law.'

## The need for a support network

Completing a degree, or any other university programme, is a serious undertaking. It demands dedication, motivation, inspiration and sheer hard work. It can therefore be stressful or overwhelming at times, especially when all the deadlines seem to come at the same moment. How do you keep all the balls in the air? It is unlikely you will complete your course without some ups and downs along the way. For this reason it is essential that you develop a good support network both to help you to be effective and to assist you through the lows and pressured times. You really do need the help of your friends, and 'friends', as this chapter shows, can be many and varied.

This network might consist of a variety of people: certainly of academic staff and staff providing student study support, as well as your fellow students, parents and maybe more. Different people will be needed in different ways and at different times during your course. Remember that early on you will cross paths with many people and it will not be immediately clear whether or how these contacts will be useful in the future.

---

### Action

The number of people and their different roles and locations make a little system a good thing here. Devising a system – maybe no more complex than a simple address book format – and keeping notes progressively will save you time and ensure that you do not overlook sources of advice and assistance.

---

# Academic staff

At university you are taught by academic staff. This includes professors, readers, senior lecturers and lecturers (we use the word 'lecturer' through-out this book to include all members of academic staff). For some parts of your course such people may be supported by research staff and research students.

Members of academic staff are usually actively pursuing a programme of research around their specialist interests. This means that they are experts in their field and you should make the most of having them around. They are your primary source of academic support while at university.

Different staff will teach different courses, according to their expertise. This means that out of all the academics with whom you come into contact you are likely to meet at least several whom you get on with and from whom you can seek support.

## The type of support available

Be clear about what is meant by 'support' here. You will not endear yourself to your lecturers if you visit them to moan about the volume of work or the imminence of an impending deadline, especially if the problem is down to your poor planning and time management. What they can give you excellent support with is things like:

- identifying the best way to tackle a problem or piece of coursework from a range of options you present;
- reviewing an early draft;

- discussing ideas and questions for essays and presentations;
- giving added guidance about suitable reading material.

But, you should keep in mind that university is not about spoon-feeding you answers. If that happened, you would not improve your own, independent thinking and analytical skills, both of which are extremely helpful qualities in the job market. What lecturers want to see is that you have been grappling with the issues and now need a bit of advice on the next step. Indeed, most lecturers will be pleased to be approached in this way and happy to help. What you need to do is develop a relationship with your lecturers so that this kind of academic interaction is a regular, constructive and natural part of your course.

## When to see lecturers

Lecturers usually have fixed office hours each week when they are available to students to answer all types of questions. Obviously, their speciality is academic issues, but you may find that you have other sorts of queries – for example over your accommodation – and be unsure of what to do next. Your lecturer probably won't have a direct answer to such questions, but they will be able to guide you to the right people for help; perhaps this is something not to overdo – always check in other ways too in case the solution is easily found. Do not be afraid to visit lecturers during these office hours. They would much rather sort out an issue or discuss ideas early on than have to sort out any difficulties with a piece of work close to the submission time.

If a lecturer's office hours clash with your other time commitments, most are very happy to arrange alternative times. However, as lecturers' time between seminars and lectures is often full of other commitments, many do not tend to appreciate students dropping by unannounced and expecting to be seen immediately. Take note: antagonizing lecturers in any way is not a good idea.

Making appointments to see lecturers or asking them initial questions is often done by e-mail, and here, again, it is useful to follow a set of simple rules. Ensure that you address your lecturer by their correct title and sign off giving your name. Before going to university few people will have come across titles like 'doctor' or 'professor' outside of trips to the health centre or hospital, but these are the usual academic titles of university staff, and it is important to get them right in communications. Unsurprisingly, students, particularly first year students, often find it quite hard to remember the names of lecturers. You walk into your first lecture or seminar, the lecturer introduces themselves, but you can easily forget to note down their name and then become embarrassed to ask as the weeks start to slip by.

Action

Take careful note of everyone who is teaching you – names, titles, hours available and so on – and then you'll be able to direct any queries to the right person. Keep notes too of queries and questions that are handled helpfully so that you can return to the good sources (or resolve to find and try others).

## How to approach lecturers

When you contact a lecturer, do not fall into the trap of communicating with them as if writing a text message to a friend. A surprising number of students send e-mails along these lines:

'Hi having probs getting essay in can have ext'

And that's it apart from the e-mail address, which might be something like **abc123@uni.ac.uk**. Receiving such messages often – understandably – riles lecturers and they are not inclined to look upon the request sympathetically. Lecturers, indeed all university staff, expect all e-mail communications to be polite and clear. Make yours so. Using such forms of communication builds up bonds between lecturers, other staff and students, which means that your interaction is friendly and informal and, crucially, helpful. All this helps you get prompt answers and keeps you ahead of the game.

## Using research staff and students for support

If you are taught by research staff or research students for parts of your course (perhaps a practical session or seminar) you may find they too make very useful contacts. They are likely to be closer to you in age, and many will have done their undergraduate degree at the same institution, so they may have been a student on the course they are now teaching on. They will understand the kind of concerns and worries that you may have.

## Tutorial groups

Most universities operate a tutorial system which allocates small groups of students to a particular lecturer at the start of their first year. The effectiveness of such groups varies enormously. Some lecturers welcome the responsibility and organize regular meetings, perhaps including social events, so that the group itself as well as the lecturer becomes a great source of support. Other lecturers are less proactive and will just say 'you're welcome to come and see me if you have a problem'. The implication of this approach may seem to be '...but I'd rather you didn't if you can possibly help it'. If this is the case then you should approach another lecturer that you know, or, alternatively, there will be academic support services outside of your department, and it is these that we will consider next.

# Academic support services

All universities have support services that provide advice on study skills and effective learning approaches and techniques for students. These are in three main areas:

- academic study skills (for example, essay writing, planning a dissertation, revision and exam technique);
- library skills (for example, using online resources, finding journal articles);
- IT skills (for example using Microsoft Word, Excel and PowerPoint, using e-mail and the internet).

These support services will have different names and be structured differently in every university, but usually you can get help both by attending a specific course and by individual assistance. Such individual assistance is usually highly tailored and specific, and can involve help with managing your time, completing assignments, and so on.

Academic support services are not a substitute for talking to your lecturers. They do different things. For example, if you want help in planning an essay, the study skills team may be able to help you develop good reading and note-taking skills, and help with essay planning. However, they cannot assist with the content or make judgements about your initial ideas and thinking. For such advice you will need to contact your lecturer.

## *Departmental study support services*

Many academic departments within universities now run specialist study support services for students. These are usually very helpful as they assist you to transform the generic skills advice into specific hints and guidance on your particular degree programme. Most of these services work on an informal, drop-in basis and run throughout the academic year. Sometimes students seem to feel ashamed of accessing these services, but it is vitally important not to look on these sessions as remedial or as a symbol of failure. Seeking advice on sharpening your study skills is the mark of a reflective, clear-thinking and committed student, and the lecturers who run these programmes are always happy to provide assistance. Increasingly, these pro-grammes also make use of other undergraduates, which can be very helpful. Knowing that there are other students out there who have experienced the same kind of study skills issues, have worked at them, and can provide advice from the same point of view can be very encouraging and supportive (see the next section on fellow students.)

## Administrative and secretarial staff

Another informal source of support in many departments is administrative and secretarial staff. Many of them can be a huge support, especially for new students, simply by being a friendly face and helping you navigate the new systems and procedures. They are adept at managing the academic staff in their department and may be able to advise you on the best way to approach a lecturer with a problem. Most academics will tell you – only half-jokingly – that it would not matter at all if they were run over by a bus one afternoon, but if it happened to one of the departmental administrative team, the whole place would grind to a halt. The administrative team keeps track of things like the overall department timetable and where all lecturers are at any given time. They liaise with other academic departments, the faculty office, and the central university administration regularly and so are at the hub of all the information which flows in and out of the department.

### Action

If you need support with issues that are broader than just academic, or have serious problems in your personal life, most universities have a counselling service which provides some (perhaps limited) free and confidential support for students. If necessary seek them out promptly; it may help prevent an awkward problem escalating.

## Fellow students

Fellow students are doubtless a disparate group. Some may be likeable, some may be daunting or difficult to work with (this was touched on in Chapter 2), but equally your fellow students can be great supporters; after all, they know exactly what you are going through, as they are experiencing similar things. Practical support and collaboration is a real possibility here; all it needs is a little organization. Some examples follow.

Top tips...

...for mutual support

Look for opportunities such as the following; such tactics can make things easier and save time:

1   swapping highly graded essays to help with revision;

2   swapping draft essays for feedback and critique;

3   sharing background reading and summarizing the main points for each other (although this cannot be a substitute for the detailed reading that is necessary for essay preparation);

4   swapping lecture notes, and clarifying areas of confusion;

5   co-operating as examination revision partners.

You can also give each other moral support when necessary. One odd example of this occurs in Singapore where students gather in public places – parks, steps to public buildings, the riverside – to study or revise in company. Favourite places vary over time. Practical, everyday support unrelated to your academic studies might be very welcome for someone trying to focus on, say, completing a dissertation before the deadline (for example, cooking a meal, getting some shopping, and so on).

Sometimes, if coursework is overwhelming but there are no imminent deadlines, the best medicine is a good night out, or in some way taking time away from your desk to clear your mind. And who is better placed to provide a break than your fellow students!

Students in the years above you can be an invaluable source of support for your studies, for example in preparing dissertations or presentations, or assisting with revision for examinations and the like. All of these things are so much less daunting once you have already been through them once, and fellow students will be able to help you move from a state of what may, at worst, be blind panic to a more systematic approach to the task in hand.

Some universities have study support networks which can provide slightly more formal student-to-student academic support.

# Student subject societies

Closely related to the support that you can get from fellow students is that from student societies related to your subject (for example History Society,

Film Society, French Society). These groups – and there are many of them – will have organized activities related to their discipline. Societies often organize things such as talks, quizzes, dinners, film shows and trips (sometimes to some exotic places). Most of these activities will enhance your studies and will do so in a fun and informal environment. In addition, such societies often ask along lecturers in order to form teams in things such as pub quizzes, and these events can then serve as excellent ways to bond academics with students still further.

---

**Action**

Check out the groups that exist, review their activities and consider carefully which may be fun, interesting or of practical help to you and which you should join.

---

## Trips

As mentioned earlier, student societies will often organize visits and, occasionally, foreign excursions. Similar things are put on by many lecturers as additional extras to their courses where such a trip is relevant to their content (for example, students on a War Studies programme might have the opportunity to visit the battlefields and cemeteries of the First World War). Of course, these trips, particularly if they are overseas, will mean a financial commitment from the student. However, the price often contains a university subsidy and so it would be far more expensive if you tried to make such trips independently. Although not crucial to passing any module, the additional understanding that visits and trips imparts, as well as the socializing aspect, can be invaluable.

---

**Action**

If you see such activities in the offing then it may be useful to check out as soon as possible how they work, where they fit in and what the time and monetary costs are – or least so that you can include those that appeal in your budgeting.

---

# Parents

If you are going away to a university straight after leaving school, it can be too easy to lose touch with home as you settle into your new life and freedom. However, your parents can be a brilliant source of support if you involve them in what is happening; so too can other members of the family circle, amongst which useful influences can easily be overlooked. University life can be very intense and focused and it is hard not to lose your sense of perspective at times. Staying in touch with the real world is important – perhaps not least because you want to return home in the holidays, and have all your cooking, cleaning and washing done for you!

# Support for mature students

Universities have embraced the idea of lifelong learning and realize that not all students will be coming straight from school. If you are a mature student it is likely that you will have other responsibilities to fit around your university work, some of which may not be flexible (such as the collection of children from school or nursery). Most universities now provide significant practical help for such students. Timetabling restrictions can be taken into account, and if not resolved, then lectures may be recorded and available as a podcast. Although there is a limit to what can be done to accommodate one individual's circumstances when large numbers of students are involved, you should find that the university will do whatever it can to support you. You may also find the Mature Students' Society another source of support.

Studying for a degree can be, at times, intense, focused and pressurized. Indeed the whole of university life can be demanding, particularly if you are living away from home for the first time. While going to university is all about learning to stand on your own two feet and develop your independence, both intellectually and in terms of wider life skills (you are, after all, now an adult), it should not be at any time an isolating or alienating experience.

## Action

Finally, something that may have only rare relevance: if you genuinely feel that the quality of support or teaching that you are receiving is of less than an acceptable standard, then universities do have what are effectively complaint procedures. Should you ever have need to use these, read the guidelines (which tend to be long and complicated) carefully. Contact the Students' Union, and get any other advice you need to ensure you tackle this the right way.

There are a plethora of structures and systems to ensure that you can get the support you need. Make sure that you use them when necessary.

---

### Read on...

In the next chapter we look at an activity that you will spend much of your time at university doing, and that is writing. We explore both the conventions of academic writing, which you will be required to learn and follow, and ways to improve the quality of your writing.

---

## Your notes

........................................................................................................

........................................................................................................

........................................................................................................

........................................................................................................

........................................................................................................

........................................................................................................

........................................................................................................

........................................................................................................

........................................................................................................

........................................................................................................

........................................................................................................

........................................................................................................

........................................................................................................

........................................................................................................

........................................................................................................

........................................................................................................

........................................................................................................

........................................................................................................

........................................................................................................

........................................................................................................

# 06
# The written word: making it work for you

**In this chapter...**

Now we turn to a **key personal skill**, one essential to university success and of prime use in career terms too. There is more to this than might immediately appear – what can seem straightforward actually demands some careful consideration; it was Somerset Maugham who said: 'All the words I use... can be found in a dictionary – it's just a matter of arranging them in the right order.' If there is one area where attention to detail pays dividends, then this is it; it's another opportunity to maximize the possibility of getting good results.

Whatever subject you study you are going to have to write coursework – essays, dissertations, reports and presentations are a major part of all university courses, and the primary means by which you will be assessed. It is critical then that you write well. Good writing, which means, not least, something that is easy to read and understand, will always be likely to get more attention, and impress more, than sloppy writing. Yet prevailing standards in this area are by no means good. Many students struggle with written coursework, at least early on.

Why is this? Maybe it is earlier education – or lack of it. Often school assists little with the kind of writing we find ourselves having to do once we move on to higher education – and additionally, academic writing has certain conventions which you need to quickly learn and follow. Maybe poor writing occurs initially because of a lack of understanding about how to go about it and lack of practice – certainly this is something that should get easier and quicker to do well as time goes on.

# A fragile process

We can all recognize the really bad essay, which fails to answer the question, is without structure or style, but has an excess of jargon, convoluted sentences, bad grammar and which prompts only the single thought: What is it trying to say? But coursework does not have to be such a complete mess to fail in its purpose. Written work is inherently fragile. Even one wrongly chosen word may dilute understanding or act to remove what would otherwise be a positive point made.

Do not underestimate this factor. Evidence of a lack of checking is all around: one computer manual states prominently at the front: 'The information presented in this publication has been carefully for reliability'; no one is infallible, but this makes a powerful point.

---

### Action

As a very first rule to drum into your subconscious, make a habit of always reading over what you write – check, check and check again. Reading your draft text out loud will highlight any problem areas.

---

# A major opportunity

Whatever the reasons for poor writing may be, suffice to say that if prevailing standards are low, then there is a major opportunity here for those who better that standard; more so for those who excel. Conversely, consistently poor writing can blight the writing even of those who know their subject well.

But you can write well. We may not all aspire to or succeed in writing the great novel, but most people can learn to turn out a good essay: writing that is clear and readable, that answers the question, uses evidence to develop their own argument persuasively and has a clear conclusion. Good essay writing need not be difficult. It is a skill, one that can be developed with study and practice. Some effort may be involved, and certainly practice helps, but it could be worse. Somerset Maugham is quoted as saying: 'There are three rules for writing the novel. Unfortunately, no one knows what they are.' The kind of writing most students must do is not so dependent on creativity, though this is involved, and it is subject to certain rules.

This chapter reviews the skills you need for academic writing. It covers both the conventions for this, and guidance on good writing. It will help you develop good writing habits from the start of your programme, and mean that writing coursework is easier and – desirable in its own right – quicker to do.

## Who are you writing for?

As a student the coursework you write is unlikely to have a wide audience. Its primary purpose is to meet the requirements of your course, and it will be read and assessed by your lecturer. Some coursework (or examination scripts) may be looked at by a second marker, or the external examiner, but all do so with the same purpose in mind: to assess your progress and see how well you have interpreted and answered the question. This will allow them to give you a mark that will feed into your final grade. You may share draft or completed coursework with friends (and some universities have essay banks), but you are not writing for them. Keep your audience and purpose in mind as you write.

# Conventions of academic writing

Like many forms of specialist writing, academic writing has a set of conventions that you need to follow when completing your coursework. These conventions include:

## *Formal language and presentation*

The style of writing you need to use for coursework is very different from that you use elsewhere. It is much more formal than e-mails and letters. When drafting your essay, use this checklist to make sure that you have avoided the dangerous pitfalls in language and grammar. Ask yourself:

**TABLE 6.1** Checklist for essay writing

| | |
|---|---|
| Have I avoided slang, colloquial terms, clichés and abbreviations? This means not using 'they're' and 'weren't' or such terms as 'eg' and 'ie' as well as clichéd and colloquial phrases such as 'To be fair' or 'At the end of the day'.... | |
| Have I used full sentences? Bullet point lists are not acceptable for most academic writing, particularly essays. | |
| Have I used correct grammar and spelling? This is important. You will not impress your lecturers if you misspell key technical information in your field. Poor grammar and spelling are inexcusable and give an overall sloppy impression. | |
| Have I avoided the use of 'I'? Instead you should use phrases such as 'As has been demonstrated above...', 'The next point to consider is...' and so on. | |

Almost all coursework is written using a computer, which certainly makes it easier to present it well. With several years of coursework ahead it may be worth working on speeding up your typing skills, something that is also likely to be useful in many a workplace. Detail is important; you should:

- Avoid using a variety of different fonts, sizes and styles throughout, which looks messy and can be hard to read.
- Use bold, italics and underlining to highlight headings (if used) or key points only where necessary, and avoid overusing these.
- Most importantly, make sure you follow any guidance from your lecturer about how they want coursework presented.

## A clear line of argument, which develops through the piece

Your writing will address a question or topic, usually set by your lecturers. You need not just to research and summarize the disparate views on the topic, but rather develop and set out your own understanding and opinion. Your writing should then develop your argument progressively, with a logical line of reasoning, and clear conclusions. (See 'Approaching an essay' on page 89.)

At this point it is also worth stressing the importance of relevance. Your text must:

- cover what is required;
- be without irrelevant content or digression.

Note: comprehensiveness is never an objective. If an essay touched on absolutely everything then it would certainly be too long. In fact, you always have to be selective; if you do not say everything, then everything you do say is a choice – you need to make good content choices, and this is one of the skills you need to develop.

## Use of evidence to support your argument

At university level it is insufficient to simply state your opinion, or even that of others. Thus:

- The statements you make in your coursework need to be evidenced through referencing other material.
- You will be unable to make a persuasive case or even to answer the question without using material from lectures, books, journal articles, websites and other sources.
- You will need to evaluate and assess this evidence (see Chapter 4) as part of developing your argument.
- You must show that you understand there are other ways to interpret the evidence and try to demonstrate where there are weaknesses in them.
- Be honest: if there are gaps or weaknesses in your own line of reasoning, you must use evidence to show why you still think your conclusions are appropriate.

## Clear references

In all academic writing you need to show the precise source of the information, arguments and ideas you use. This is true whether or not you quote directly from the other work. As was shown in Chapter 4, university-level study demands that you develop your own ideas and critical thinking. It is fundamental to this that you do not try to pass off other people's ideas and arguments as your own (doing this is called plagiarism, see box). Therefore the convention of referencing is used to show where the ideas come from.

There are other benefits to referencing too. It allows readers to refer back to the source themselves if they wish. (As shown in Chapter 4, it may be that other readers will interpret the same material differently from you.) Using references like this is one way that you can make your argument persuasive; it shows that you have evidence to back up what you are saying. Using a wide range of well-chosen references will also demonstrate the thoroughness of your research.

### Plagiarism

Plagiarism, or passing off someone else's work as your own, is a major offence (and may also involve breach of copyright and copyright law). It includes:

- quoting or paraphrasing another person's work without acknowledgement;

- using ideas or arguments developed by another without acknowledgement.

Plagiarism is likely to lead to you receiving a zero for the particular piece of coursework involved and, if you persist, it could even mean that you are not allowed to continue your course. Lecturers are used to identifying plagiarism in student coursework, however cleverly it is disguised.

Don't even think about it!

### Action

To make sure you can reference other works accurately, and avoid plagiarism, it is important that you keep good notes as you research. As you will need to study a wide range of material, you will quickly lose track of which ideas came from where if you are not careful.

## Referencing

When referencing material within the text of your coursework it is sufficient to include just the author and year (for example '...the argument developed by Jones (1994)...' or '...the Jaffa Cake theory demonstrates (Jones, 1994)...') so as not to break the flow of the text. A footnote or endnote is then used to give the full reference:

- the author's name;
- the full title (in italics or underlined for a book, in single quotation marks for a journal article);
- year of publication;
- journal name (in italics or underlined) and issue number (if applicable);
- name and location of publisher;

- page numbers;
- webpage address (if applicable);
- any other information that is needed to allow someone else to find the material.

For example, Connelly and Forsyth, P., *The Study Skills Guide*, Kogan Page, London, 2010, p. 86

Some subjects may have slightly different conventions for referencing and it is important that you find out what the norm is in your field.

If you quote directly from the source the relevant part should be put in quotation marks, or, if it is a very long piece, in a separate, indented, paragraph (without quotation marks), like this:

Plagiarism, or passing off someone else's work as your own, is a major offence. It includes:

- quoting or paraphrasing another person's work without acknowledgement;
- using ideas or arguments developed by another without acknowledgement.

Plagiarism is likely to lead to you receiving a zero for the particular piece of coursework involved and, if you persist, it could even mean that you are not allowed to continue your course. Lecturers are used to identifying plagiarism in student coursework, however cleverly it is disguised.

Don't even think about it! (Connelly & Forsyth, 2010, p. 86)

## *Word limit*

Whatever type of coursework you are doing there will be a word count target. If a lecturer asks for 2,000 words it is because they believe that will allow you to do justice to the subject. Delivering 1,000 or 5,000 words is not likely to be well regarded. However, you are not, of course, expected to hit the word limit exactly and you can normally work on the basis of about 10 per cent or so leeway either way, though this can vary somewhat and it is useful to check.

# What makes for 'good' writing?

In an academic setting the first thing is to address the assignment accurately. If you need to write a review of something, contrast and compare differing viewpoints or analyse the truth of some contention, then do just that. Content matters. But with content addressed, the writing must enhance it.

Generally, communication is inclined to be less than straightforward. This is true of tiny communications: there is a notice on Paddington station that says

'Passengers must not leave their luggage unattended or they will be taken away and destroyed.' This is just one sentence. How much more potential for misunderstanding does a 2,000-word essay present? And with written communication the danger is that any confusion lasts. Once an essay is submitted that is that; it is not a conversation where you can adapt what you say in light of any inadequacies in what you first say.

The rest of this chapter therefore focuses on helping you write well, that is, clearly, persuasively and succinctly. First we consider an example of the good/bad essay, then we turn to a systematic approach to writing and then to how to use language clearly.

# Structure

Different types of academic writing will have different structures, but for each type there will be a standard structure which you need to identify and follow. Below we examine the basic structure for the most common form of academic writing, the essay.

## Example essay structure

1   Title: The essay title is a key part of the essay itself. Make sure you understand and stick to the question asked.

2   Introduction: Explore the essay question or title, make your line of argument clear, summarize your conclusion and state briefly the evidence you are going to examine to demonstrate this.

3   Main part of essay: Here you develop your argument. Break different ideas down into paragraphs, making sure there is a logical sequence from each one to the next, and that overall a persuasive line of reasoning is developed. This is the most complex part of the essay and this arrangement needs pre-planning (more of this later).

4   Conclusion: Summarize the main ideas in your essay (don't introduce any new ideas at this stage), clearly stating your own conclusions, and showing why these are important. This must be precise and yet succinct (an example follows).

5   References: References may be in the form of footnotes throughout the essay, or endnotes as suggested by this example structure. More details on the convention of referencing were mentioned earlier.

6 Bibliography: Don't make the mistake of thinking this is an extra or add-on section. The bibliography is a core part of the essay. Here you should list:

- All the books, journal articles and other evidence you have consulted in answering the question, even those that you have not taken references from.

- The full bibliographic details of each piece in the same format as you have done for references. Order the bibliography alphabetically, using the surname of the author.

- And beware: do not be tempted to include items that you have not referred to – their content, when compared to your essay, may make it clear that you are bluffing.

# Approaching an essay

It is likely that you will have a choice of essay questions, and so considering each one before making your final selection is critical. Make sure you understand the question and choose a topic that interests you as you will spend a long time working on it.

Before you begin this actual work, it is essential that you understand the question that you are answering. Think carefully about the question and consider any keywords which will help you plan your response. Most essay titles or questions are relatively formulaic. The main types are:

| | |
|---|---|
| Evaluate | Consider the value of something (or a range of things), exploring its strengths and weaknesses, and arriving at a firm conclusion in your assessment. |
| Compare and contrast | Place two or more things in relative perspective. Highlight similarities and differences, showing why these are significant. (This is often a favourite term in examination questions as it forces you to demonstrate a breadth of knowledge.) |
| Analyse, examine, explain or discuss | Explore something in depth to show your awareness of different interpretations, ability to identify and assess key issues. |
| Consider to what extent | Determine the degree of importance or impact of something upon an outcome or argument. |

## Essays – the good, the bad and the downright useless

Given that the average student essay is in excess of 2,000 words, it is not possible to include a complete text in this book, much less one reflecting every course universities offer. Instead we have picked a topic and provided a sample 'good' and 'bad' introduction and conclusion to demonstrate some of the main issues to be aware of.

The student has been answering the following essay question: 'Can any one factor be identified as the cause of the First World War?'

## Introduction

### Good

Historians have argued over the causes of the First World War since the 1920s. Over the decades many complex arguments have been created to explain why Europe fell into war in 1914. In the immediate aftermath of war the Germans were held responsible for the disaster. Gradually this gave way to the idea of collective responsibility shared among the great powers of Europe. However, in the 1960s the German historian, Fritz Fischer, controversially returned the debate to its origins by once again emphasizing the primacy of Germany in the outbreak of war. Within the immense spectrum of arguments on the cause of the conflict are historians who have singled out one particular factor while others have argued that a range of factors combined to create disaster. This essay will explore the main schools of thought concerning the causes of the war, placing particular emphasis on those who have blamed Germany and those who see it as a disaster either unwittingly or consciously brought about by the great powers.

### Bad

This essay is about the causes of the First World War. There is much debate about the causes of the war with some saying that it was down to the navy rivalry and some saying that it was about empires. Others have said it was about domestic issues. Exploring these ideas is a challenging task. In this essay I will try to identify who caused the disaster.

What does the good Introduction do?

1 It uses clear and precise language throughout.

2 It shows an awareness of the fact that the arguments and debates on issues and facts change and develop over time.

3 It moves logically from one point to another.

**4** It tells the reader clearly what the essay will do and what they can expect.

What does the bad Introduction do?

**1** It has no structure – ideas and themes are thrown about without context.

**2** It uses the personal pronoun.

**3** It does not provide sufficient detail, and immediately suggests inadequate research.

## Conclusion

*Good*

This essay has covered all of the main schools of thought concerning the causes of the First World War. It has been shown that historical interpretations have changed considerably over time. Although the primacy of German guilt has been a constant thread in the arguments, it has been demonstrated that most leading historians in the field now see the causes of the war as immensely complex and overlapping, and that Europe slithered into war in 1914 not by design but by accident. Some would argue that this accident came about only because of earlier deliberately calculated aggressive posturing. This piece has argued that the 'war by accident' approach is the most convincing by carefully comparing and contrasting the strengths and weaknesses of the varying opinions on an issue which is unlikely ever to reach a final, definitive conclusion.

*Bad*

Many things caused the First World War, and although others can be considered guilty Germany was probably mostly to blame. There are different views on the war with some saying that one nation was the cause and others saying that lots of factors were. The war was about many things and the nations fought for different reasons. The war proved tragic and futile. Finding the real cause is hard as there are so many views, but Germany seems responsible.

What does the good conclusion do?

**1** It reminds the reader clearly and succinctly what has been covered in the essay.

**2** It demonstrates the complexity of analysis and breadth of research carried out.

**3** It shows awareness of alternative views, but comes to a firm conclusion through a rational and rigorous process.

What does the bad conclusion do?

1   There is no definite conclusion and no sense of argument developed.

2   It uses emotive language ('guilty', 'tragic', 'futile') that simply expresses a personal view and makes an inappropriate judgement for an academic essay (and the statement is not relevant to the question set).

3   The references to secondary literature are unclear and vague.

Of course, the main body of the essay must also proceed logically and reflect what is promised in the introduction. Remember too that the quality of any essay can be diluted by poor use of language, an element that is addressed elsewhere in this chapter.

# A systematic approach

A good essay is unlikely to spill out of you perfectly formed. It needs some thought and benefits from the adoption of a systematic approach: that is, one proceeding a step at a time, and logically moving through to the desired end result.

So, to encompass all possibilities and degrees of complexity, the following seven-stage approach sets out a methodology that will cope with any kind of document (it is the way this book began life, too). It is recommended only by its practicality. It works. It will make your writing quicker and easier to do and more impressive. It can instil the right habits and rapidly become something you can work with, utilizing its methods more or less comprehensively depending on the circumstances.

## *Stage 1: Listing*

This consists of ignoring all thoughts about sequence or structure, and simply listing every significant point which might be desirable or necessary to include (though perhaps bearing in mind the nature and length of the essay and the level of detail involved). To give us an example, let's refer back to Chapter 1: imagine you have to write an essay on managing your time (you might if you do a management course though here the brief is a simple how-to one). The initial 'list' might look like the box shown in Figure 6.1.

This, a process that draws on what is sometimes called 'mind-mapping', gets all the elements involved down on paper. It may need more than one session to complete it; certainly you will find one thought leading to another as the picture fills out. Rather than set this out as a neat list down the page, it is better to adopt a freestyle approach.

**FIGURE 6.1**    Example of 'freestyle' approach to this stage of preparation

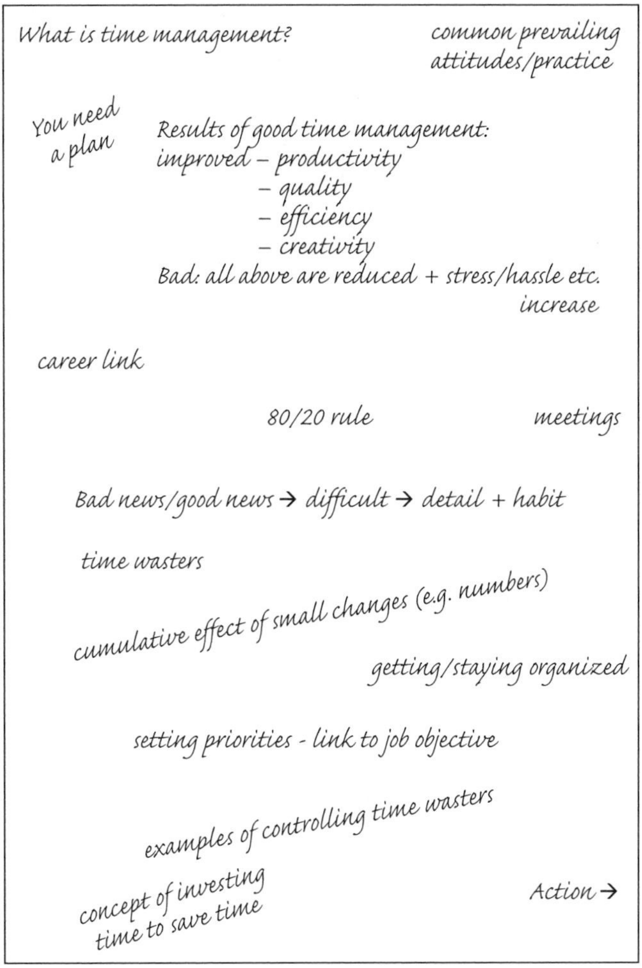

What is time management?                    common prevailing
                                            attitudes/practice

You need
a plan        Results of good time management:
              improved – productivity
                       – quality
                       – efficiency
                       – creativity
              Bad: all above are reduced + stress/hassle etc.
                                            increase

career link

                    80/20 rule                    meetings

Bad news/good news → difficult → detail + habit

time wasters

cumulative effect of small changes (e.g. numbers)

                    getting/staying organized

setting priorities - link to job objective

examples of controlling time wasters

concept of investing
time to save time                    Action →

In this way, points are noted, almost at random, around a sheet. This allows you to end up able to view the totality of your notes in one glance, so if necessary you should use a sheet larger than standard A4 paper. It is also best done on paper, not on screen (the next stages make clear why).

## Stage 2: Sorting

Next, you can proceed to rearrange what you have noted and bring some logic and organization to bear on it. This process may raise some questions as well as answer others, so it is still not giving you the final shape of the essay. This

**FIGURE 6.2** Sorting: example of this stage of preparation

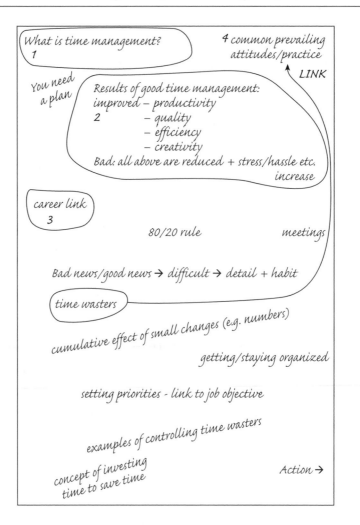

stage is often best (and most quickly) done by annotating the original list. A second colour pen may help now as you begin to put things in order, make logical groupings and connections, as well as allowing yourself to add and subtract points and refine the total picture as you go. Figure 6.2 extends the example from the first stage (you must imagine a second colour).

## Stage 3: Arranging

This stage arranges your 'jottings' into a final order of contents, and here you can decide upon the precise sequence and arrangements you will follow for the text itself. For the sake of neatness, and thus to give yourself a clear guideline to follow as you move on, it is often worth rewriting the sheet you were left with after stage 2 (indeed, this is the point to transfer onto computer screen if you wish).

At this stage you can also form a view and note specifically the emphasis that will be involved. For example: What is most important? Where is most detail necessary? What needs illustrating? (This may involve anything from a graph to an example.) What will take most space?

Not enough material? Usually the reverse is true. And this is the stage at which to prune, if necessary, so that what is included is well chosen, but not inappropriately long. This is true at all levels. Contain the number of points to be made and the amount to be said about each. Of course, you need to write sufficient to match your purpose, but do not risk submerging it in a plethora of irrelevant detail or subsidiary points that are actually unnecessary digressions. The example continues in the box.

---

### Time management

- Common problems – results: less (productivity etc)/more: (stress, hassle etc)

- Makes a difference to working practices and results

- Fact of life: 80/20 rule – 20% of your time produces 80% of results

- What makes it difficult? (no magic formula... success is in the detail)

- What makes it easier: establishing good habits

- You need a plan – and a diary system

- Deciding priorities

- Controlling time wasters – yourself and other people (meetings)

- Action for the future.

---

## Stage 4: Review

At this point, have a final look over what you now plan to do – review your 'arranged' guideline. It will be quicker and easier to make final amendments now than when you finally print out pages of draft. It may help to 'sleep on it', carrying out a final review having distanced yourself from what you have done so far, at least for a moment. You can easily get so close to something that you are working hard at, that you cannot see the wood for the trees. One of the things you want to be clear about is the broad picture – if this is right, then the details will slot into place much more easily.

Do not worry if you still want to make amendments at this stage. Add things, delete things, move things about (rewrite your guidelines if necessary) – but make sure that when you move on to write something you do so confident that the outline represents your considered view of the content and will act as a really useful guide.

Let us be clear: for many a document this whole process (ie stages 1–4) will take only a few minutes, and that is time well spent, as it will reduce the time taken once you start to write. As you develop your own style of this sort of preparation, you will find you can shorthand the process a little, with some documents able to be written from the first freehand-style list. If real complexity is involved, of course, it may take longer.

With all that has been done to date, it is now time to write; and you are now able to do so, having separated deciding what to write (at this stage largely done) from how to write it. This is significant and makes matters easier and faster. So next:

## Stage 5: Write

What else is there to say? This stage means writing it. This is the bit with the greatest element of chore in it. But it has to be done and the guidelines you have given yourself by preparing carefully will ease and speed the process. A few practical tips may also help, see box.

---

**Top tips...**

### ...for getting the words down

- Choose the right moment. We certainly find there are moments when we cannot seem to... when we are unable... when it is difficult... to string two coherent sentences together end to end. There are other times when things flow, when you do not dare stop in case the flow does too, and when you cannot get the words down fast enough to keep up with your thoughts.

- Do not struggle. If possible (although deadlines may have an effect here), do not struggle. If it is really not flowing – leave things. Stop. For a moment, overnight, or while you walk round the block or make a cup of tea. Many people confirm that when the words simply will not flow, a pause helps.

- Allow sufficient time; once you are under way and words are flowing smoothly it may upset and slow the process to leave it. If you feel you need an uninterrupted day, or more, try to organize things that way. It may both save time in the long run and help you produce better text.

- Do not stop unnecessarily. For example, when you get stuck over some – maybe important – detail. Say you need to decide on a heading or a phrase, one which must be clear, pithy and fit with the style of the whole thing. You just cannot think of one. Leave it, type some xxxxs and write on. You can always come back to it (and when you do, who knows, you sometimes think of just what you want in a moment). The danger is that you dither, puzzle over it, waste time, get nowhere, but get so bogged down with it that you lose everything you had in your mind about the overall shape of what you are working on. This is true of words, phrases, sentences and even whole sections. Mark clearly what you need to come back to (so that you never forget to check it again!).

That said, the job here is to get the whole thing down on paper. It probably will not be perfect, but you should not feel bad about that; a vanishingly small number of people can create any document word for word exactly as they want it first time. Practice will get you closer and closer, and things you are familiar with will be easier than something that is new to you or pushes your knowledge or expertise to the limits.

### Action

One idea many find useful and which you should consider is to handwrite some of your written work. Why? Because you cannot use a computer in an examination and suddenly having to handwrite something when you are used to typing may be a shock to the system, one making writing slower and more difficult; content quality can suffer because of this. A few drafts done this way will give you practice.

But some revision is usually necessary; hence the next stage.

## Stage 6: Edit

The complexities of the material you are using and the arguments you are developing mean that some editing is almost always necessary. There are a number of points here that help make this stage practical but not protracted; again the box expands on this with some practical suggestions.

## Top editing tips

- If possible, leave a draft for a while before rereading it. You get very close to something and, without a pause, start to see only what you expect (or hope) is there. It is often much quicker to finish off something in this way than trying to undertake the whole job with one stage back to back with the next.

- Read things over, out loud is best (though choose where!). You will hear how something sounds and that reflects how it will feel to read. When you do this, you will find that certain things – such as overlong sentences – jump out at you very clearly (you run out of breath).

- Get a fellow student to read it. A fresh look often casts light on areas you have convinced yourself are fine, for no other reason than you cannot think of a better way of expressing something (co-authorship certainly proves the worth of this idea!). Some students habitually do this on a swap basis. Because review can be time-consuming, they ask a view of one thing in return for doing the same for someone else. This can work well; better if you do it regularly.

- Worry about the detail. It was Oscar Wilde who said: 'I was working on the proof of one of my poems all the morning, and took out a comma. In the afternoon I put it back.' Actually the small details are important. For example, you may create greater impact by breaking a sentence into two, with a short one following a longer one. It makes a more powerful point. See.

- Look at the structure. Now that all your points are developed in detail, does it work effectively? Would moving one particular point or paragraph elsewhere help your line of reasoning develop more logically?

Editing is an important stage. If you need to read it over three times, so be it. Of course, you could perhaps go on making changes for ever and finally you have to let something go. But more than one look will be essential.

## Stage 7: Proof-read

Once you have a final draft it is critical that you proof-read it. Make sure you use a spellchecker, but remember they are not infallible. If possible, use a grammar checker too.

In terms of time, spending time on preparation will reduce writing time. Similarly, it is usually more time efficient to crack through a draft and then make some changes, rather than labour over trying to make every line perfect as you first write. Like much that is involved here, habit plays a part. What matters is to find an approach for working through all of this that suits you, and prompts a thorough job that produces the end result you want.

---

**Action**

Using (perhaps having fine-tuned the approach) a systematic approach really does make writing easier and quicker. It may need a small effort to get into this, but the effort is worthwhile and you will quickly feel the benefit. Tackle your next writing assignment this way and see.

---

# Using clear language

If you undertake to engender a totality of meaning which corresponds with the cognition of others seeking to intake a communication from the content you display in an essay there is a greater likelihood of results being less than you hope.

You are correct. That is not a good start. If we want to say: if you write well, people will understand and be more likely to mark you accordingly – then we should say just that. But it makes a good point with which to start this section. Language and how you use it matter. Exactly how you put things has a direct bearing on how they are received; and that in turn has a direct bearing on how well an essay reads and how it will be marked.

Habit, and the ongoing pressure of work, can combine to push people into writing on 'automatic pilot'. Sometimes, if you critique something that you wrote you can clearly see something that is wrong. A sentence does not make sense, a point fails to get across or a description confuses rather than clarifies. Usually the reason that this has occurred is not that you really thought this was the best sentence or phrase and got it wrong. Rather it was because there was inadequate thought of any sort – or none at all as you rushed.

It is clear language that makes a difference. But this is a serious understatement; language can make a very considerable difference. And it can make a difference in many different ways, as we intend to show. Think of text you must read. What makes something good or bad, easy to read or hard work? In considering the next section here, it might help to look at an example and make a list. Certainly matters like using the right words, arrangement of words, grammar and punctuation and a straightforward approach all help.

Here we consider matters under three broad headings. Readers want documents to be understandable, readable and straightforward.

## *Understandable*

Once something is in writing, any error that causes misunderstanding is made permanent, at least for a while. The necessity for clarity may seem to go without saying, though some, at least, of what one sees of prevailing standards suggests the opposite. It is all too easy to find everyday examples of wording that is less than clear. For example:

- A favourite is a sign you see in some shops: EARS PIERCED, WHILE YOU WAIT. There is some other way? Maybe there has been a new technological development.

- Or consider this example quoted in the national press recently. The item commented that a company envisioned: 'A world where economic activity is ubiquitous, unbounded by the traditional definitions of commerce and universal'. Er, yes – or rather, no. The newspaper referred not to the content of the release, only to the fact that it contained a statement so wholly gobbledegook as to have no meaning at all. It is sad when the writing is so bad that it achieves less than nothing, and if a presumably carefully crafted document like a press release can be this inadequate, so can your essays.

You could doubtless extend such a list of examples extensively. The point here is clear: it is all too easy for the written word to fail. Such examples were probably the subject of some thought and checking; but not enough. Put pen to paper and you step onto dangerous ground.

So, beyond the link to academic study the first requirement of good writing is clarity. A good essay needs thinking about (which is what a systematic approach to writing allows, indeed prompts) if it is to be clear, and it should never be taken for granted that understanding will be automatically generated by what we write. The following factors help clarity immensely:

1 Using the right words. For example:

- Is your work on an essay continuous (unbroken or uninterrupted) or continual (repeated or recurring) – unless you never sleep it is likely to be the latter.

- Are you uninterested in a proposal or disinterested in it? The first implies you are apathetic and care not either way, the latter means you have nothing to gain from it.

- Similarly, dissatisfied and unsatisfied should not be confused. The first means disappointed and the second needing more of something.

- Fortuitous implies something happening accidentally; it does not mean fortunate.

- If something is practical then it is effective, if something is practicable it is merely possible to do, and pragmatic is something meant to be effective (rather than proven to be so).

2 Selecting and arranging words to ensure your meaning is clear. For example:

- Saying 'At this stage, the case is...' implies that later it will be something else when this might not be intended.

- Saying 'After working late into the night, the essay will be with you this afternoon' seems to imply (because of the sequence and arrangement of words) that it is the essay that was working late.

3 Good use of paragraphs: a paragraph is simply a subdivision of the text and is likely to be several sentences long. Follow this basic outline when drafting paragraphs:

- Paragraph 1: Fully explain your point or central idea and briefly contextualize.

- Paragraph 2: Provide evidence to support your point (eg reference primary or secondary sources, and explain why this supports your idea).

- Paragraph 3: Provide an example showing how your idea has been applied. This could be textual analysis, data etc. This clear evidence shows you have fully understood and developed the concept.

Point to consider: Paragraphs tend to be longer in academic essays than in magazines and newspapers, as they are more detailed and less 'punchy'. Having said that, it is the coherence of ideas that form a paragraph and not its appearance.

The first sentence makes clear that something new is being said, the middle sentences explain it and the last links on to the next paragraph and the next part of the essay.

## *Readable*

Readability is difficult to define, but we all know it when we experience it. For instance:

- Your writing must flow.
- One point must lead naturally to another.
- The writing must strike the right tone.
- You must inject a little variety.
- Above all, there must be a logical, and visible, structure to carry the message along.

As well as a clear beginning, middle and end, the technique of 'signposting' – briefly flagging what is to come – helps in a practical sense to get the reader understanding where something is going. So you might use a phrase like 'In the next section I will deal with X, Y and Z', then taking each in turn. It allows your lecturer to read on, content that the direction is sensible. It is difficult to overuse signposting and it can be utilized at several levels within the text, for instance to flag the nature of what is coming, say an example, as well as content.

Good punctuation contributes to readability: too little is exhausting to read, especially coupled with long sentences. Too much seems affected and awkward. Certain rules do matter here, but the simplest guide is probably breathing. We learn to punctuate speech long before we write anything, so in writing, all that is really necessary is a conscious inclusion of the pauses. The length of pause and the nature of what is being said indicate the likely solution. In some ways too much is better than not enough.

Do not underestimate the contribution to a successful piece of writing that careful, correct language can make. If you feel you fall short of what is necessary, it is worth some time to correct and improve your style (certainly see action box below). The boxed paragraph gives some examples and is included to reinforce the importance of this area.

## Get it write (sic)

What about grammar, syntax and punctuation? The fact that they matter has been mentioned, so does spelling, but spellcheckers largely make up for any inadequacies in that area these days (though remember that they will not be there in examinations). But care is necessary and good writing can assist understanding and your rating.

Certain things can jar; and you should be particularly careful to avoid things that examiners and lecturers will notice and dislike. Some mistakes are very obvious. For example, a few disparate points are mentioned here to show the kind of thing to watch out for:

- Poor punctuation: too little is exhausting to read, especially coupled with long sentences. Too much seems affected and awkward. Certain rules do matter here, but the simplest guide is probably breathing (mentioned earlier).

- Incorrect and annoying: some things, for whatever reason, are both wrong and annoying. A good example of this is the use of the word 'unique'. Unique means unlike anything else and so you must not write 'very unique' or 'rather unique'.

- Tautology (unnecessary repetition), of which the classic example is people who say 'I, myself personally', is to be avoided. Do not export overseas, simply export, do not indulge in forward planning, simply plan.

- Oxymorons (word combinations that are contradictory) may sound silly – distinctly foggy – or be current good ways of expressing something – deafening silence. Some sentences can cause similar problems of contradiction – 'I never make predictions; and I never will.'

We will resist digressing at length, but we intend these examples make a valuable and easily overlooked point: think on and write right.

---

### Action

Every student needs a good dictionary, thesaurus and a good grammar guide as well (something like *The Good Word Guide* (Bloomsbury). Get such and use them regularly and wisely.

---

## Straightforward

It is important to keep your essay simple and easy to read. Consider the following points when writing your essay:

- Short words: why elucidate something when you can explain? Why reimbursements rather than expenses? Similarly, although 'experiment' and 'test' do have slightly different meanings, in a general sense 'test' may be better; or you could use 'try'.

- Short phrases: do not say 'at this moment in time' when you mean now, or 'respectfully acknowledge' something, a suggestion perhaps, when you can simply say 'thank you'.

- Short sentences: having too many overlong sentences is a frequent characteristic of much poor writing, from essays to business reports. Short ones are good. However, they should be mixed in with longer ones, or reading becomes rather like the action of a machine gun. Many student essays contain sentences that are overlong, often because they mix two rather different points. Break these into two and the overall readability improves.

Of course, the content of your essays will be anything but simple. The important thing here is to have the appropriate level of detail; avoiding unnecessary complexity and jargon while dealing fully with the intricacies of the subject in simple language is a skill to work on.

Linked to this is the need to be succinct, so that your argument, case study or information is described without undue wandering before you find the right words.

# Personal style

Finally, most people have, or develop, a way of writing that includes stylistic things they simply like. Why not indeed? For example, although the rule books now say they are simply alternatives, some people think that to say: First,... secondly... and thirdly..., has much more elegance than beginning: Firstly... The reason why matters less than achieving a consistent effect you feel is right.

It would be a duller world if we all did everything the same way and writing is no exception. There is no harm in using some things for no better reason than that you like them. It is likely to add variety to your writing, and make it seem distinctively different from that of other people, which may itself be useful.

Certainly you should always be happy that what you write sounds right. So, to quote the late writer Keith Waterhouse: 'If... a sentence still reads awkwardly, then what you have there is an awkward sentence. Demolish it and start again.'

## Action

Good habits are as powerful as are bad. Almost certainly you are going to have to change your writing habits. Making a shift to new ways is possible and the rewards make the game very much worth the candle: you'll write quicker and more easily and it will ensure that your coursework is immediately understood by lecturers. Make your next essay a starting point.

## Read on....

The next area is closely aligned in some ways to writing; it is that of making a formal presentation. For instance, an essay and a presentation both need to be prepared in a similar way. Being 'on your feet' can be daunting, and it is certainly not something to launch into without careful consideration; but, well done, it is – as you will see – another opportunity to shine.

# Your notes

# 07
# Presenting successfully

**In this chapter...**

Many people are fearful, or at least uncertain, about any form of **public speaking**. An old saying puts it well: 'The human brain is a wonderful thing. It starts working the moment you are born and never stops until you stand up to speak in public' (Sir George Jessel). Yet, presenting is an inherent part of most university courses; here you will learn how to allay fears and make the most of what is undoubtedly another opportunity to enhance your performance.

## Why are students asked to give presentations?

Presentation – formal 'on your feet' presentation – is a regular part of many courses. The number and nature of presentations you will be expected to give will depend upon the course that you are following. Students in business schools, for example, may be expected to deliver regular formal presentations and groups of students may be asked to report back on a project that they have worked on collectively. It is very unlikely that you will reach the end of your course without having been asked to deliver a number of presentations. Often these will be part of the assessment process and so presenting successfully is a key skill to learn.

# Types of presentation

The type of presentation may vary, though the principles of what makes one work are similar; typical is a short – possibly 10–20 minute – informal presentation in a seminar group to kick-start the discussion on a particular topic. Typically, each student will take responsibility for one or more topics. The audience therefore includes your fellow students, but also your seminar leader or lecturer.

# How to stand out from the crowd

Giving a presentation may prompt fears, and seem daunting. It is possible that this is not something you have had to do before, and so this may well be the first time you have had to speak in public. It is likely that the topic will also be new to you and not something that you are an expert in already. But presentations are a great opportunity to shine, if done well. Furthermore, they say a great deal about you. You want to make the most of them and be able to do so manageably. Indeed, presenting is a career skill, one necessary in many jobs, useful throughout life and well worth acquiring.

Prevailing standards are not great, so standing out from the crowd is not difficult. Many people, told they must make a presentation, click on PowerPoint, knock out some slides and end up reading the inappropriately lengthy text on them verbatim; at worst they do so while standing with their back to the group and facing the screen. The phrase 'death by PowerPoint' is firmly in the language. Most of what makes for a good presentation is common sense, though there is a degree of organization – perhaps orchestration is a better word – involved. Always remember that presenting puts you in a powerful position. If you can calm any nerves that threaten to interfere, then you can think positively about it and that will help you achieve what you want.

Reassure yourself that if you do the research, investigation or project which will always precede presenting, you will know more about the topic than your fellow students at least. Show respect for your audience by having confidence in your subject and being keen to impart your new-found knowledge – not least because next week it will be their turn and whatever you learn about that topic will in part be down to them.

# A significant opportunity

There are few skills more worth mastering than that of presentation; without them you not only feel exposed, you are exposed. The trouble is the ground does not mercifully open up and allow you to disappear along with your embarrassment. It is more likely that the result is much more real – you feel inadequate and are marked accordingly. Indeed, it is all too possible for good work to be marked down because it is poorly presented; unfair perhaps, but it is how things are.

There are good reasons for having fears, but all can be either overcome or reduced to stop them overpowering your ability to work successfully. It may help to think of things as a balance:

- On one side there are things that can, unless dealt with, reduce your ability to make a good presentation.
- On the other there are techniques that positively assist the process. The right attention to both sides improves your capability.

Much of this chapter is about the positive techniques. But let us start with a little more about possible difficulties, some of which are inherent to the process, and how to overcome them, if only to get the negative side out of the way first.

# The hazards of being 'on your feet'

We all communicate so much we tend to take it for granted. Indeed, we regard much of it as easy, and unthinkingly assume we can 'wing it'.

With most presentations you only get one crack at it, and often there is not the to and fro nature of conversation that establishes understanding. 'Winging it' really isn't an option.

This means that every tiny detail matters. Presentations are inherently fragile. Small differences – an ill-chosen word or phrase, a hesitation, a misplaced emphasis – can all too easily act to dilute the impact sought. You must work at getting this right.

## *Presenters' nightmares*

The top quoted fears, in no particular order, are as follows, listed here with some thought about overcoming them:

| Fears about presenting | Tips for overcoming fears |
|---|---|
| **1. Butterflies in the stomach:** if you are nervous, then you are likely to appear nervous. Without *some* apprehension, which can act to focus you on the job in hand, you would probably not do so well. Much of this feeling will fade as you get under way (and knowing this from practice helps), but you can help the process in a number of ways. | • Taking some deep breaths before you start (nerves tend to make you breathe more shallowly and starve you of oxygen), and remember to breathe as you go along (running out of breath to the point of gasping is a surprisingly common fault).<br>• Taking a sip of water just before you start.<br>• Not eating a heavy meal before a presentation.<br>• Nor eating nothing (or rumbles may join the butterflies).<br>• Alcohol (except possibly in extreme moderation) really does not help; at worst it may persuade you that you can do something you cannot and make matters worse as the truth dawns. |
| **2. A dry mouth** | This is easily cured. Take a sip of water. Never attempt to speak without a glass or bottle of water in front of you. Even if you do not touch it, knowing it is there is a comfort. And beware of fashionable fizzy water, which can have distracting side effects! |
| **3. Not knowing what to do with your hands** | The best solution is to give your hands something to do – hold your notes, or a lectern if there is one, a pencil or the remote control for your slides, make the occasional gesture – but then forget about them. Take care: *thinking* about them as you proceed may make matters worse. |
| **4. Not knowing how loud to speak** | Just imagine you are speaking to the most distant person in the room (if they were the only one there you would have little problem judging it); better still test it beforehand. |

| Fears about presenting | Tips for overcoming fears |
| --- | --- |
| **5. A hostile reaction** | The vast majority of groups want it to go well; yet worrying that they are somehow 'against you' is a common fear. There are only a limited number of things that can go wrong. Consider what they might be and prepare for the worst:<br><br>• If you lose your place in your notes, be prepared to talk without them.<br>• If the audience looks confused, invite them to ask questions.<br>• If the audience talks over you, your teacher will be on hand to quieten them down.<br>• If you are asked a question to which you don't know the answer offer to find out later and take down their e-mail address. |
| **6. Not having sufficient material** | This can be removed completely as a fear; if your presentation is well prepared you will *know* there is the right amount (see page 116 'Rules of preparation'). |
| **7. Losing your place** | Your notes should be organized specifically so that it is unlikely that you will lose your place (and so that you can find it easily should you do so). |
| **8. Hesitating or grinding to a halt** | Dry mouth? Take a sip of water. Lose your place? Organize it so that this does not happen. Or is it just nerves? Well, some of the factors already mentioned will help – so too will preparation. And if it does happen, often it takes only a second to resume: *There was another point here, ah yes, the questions of* ... The problem here can be psychological; it just *feels* as if you paused forever. |

> **Action**
>
> Address any fears you may have. All that is necessary for most such problems or thoughts is a practical response, something that acts certainly to remove or reduce the adverse effect. Thinking of it this way helps too. Try not to worry. No doom and gloom. It will be more likely to go well if you are sure it will do so – more so if you work at organizing matters so that every factor helps. You may want to add to the list of fears above on a more personal basis.

Above all, get into the habit of speaking in seminars. Don't be the student who is always so nervous that their state is obvious to everyone else. A student who is used to speaking up in seminars, contributing their thoughts and working hypotheses through with the others will always be less nervous when it comes to presenting more formally.

But few people can speak without some thought. It was the author Mark Twain who said that it usually takes three weeks to prepare a good impromptu speech. Preparation provides a necessary foundation to success and it is to that which we turn to next.

## Preparing to present

Imagine that you have a presentation to make.

> **Action**
>
> Maybe you have a presentation to be done soon. If so, then you may find it useful to keep the details to hand as you read this chapter, using it as an example to link the points made here to your own pending task.

Only the truly foolhardy will simply do nothing about it until the day and then get up and speak. So what do you do? Let us address some dangers first to lead into what is best practice here. What you might do is think of what you want to say first, then think of what follows – what you will say second, third and so on – and then write it down verbatim. Then, perhaps after some judicious amendment, you read it to the group you must address.

Wrong, wrong and wrong again. This might sound logical, but contains the seeds of disaster. We will suggest some alternative approaches as we continue. As it is a straightforward factor to address, let us take the reading aspect first.

## Do not try to read verbatim

Some people think, at least until they have more experience, that having every word down on paper and reading them out acts as a form of security blanket. This is particularly tempting when the topic is relatively new to you and you do not have a complete grip on how all the material fits together. After all, what can go wrong if you have everything, right down to the last comma, in black and white in front of you? Well, several things in particular:

- First, you will find it is really very difficult to read anything smoothly, get all the emphasis exactly where it needs to be, and do so fluently and without stumbling. The actors that record novels, and other books, as audio works deserve their pay cheques: real skill is involved here.

- Most people speak very much better from notes which are an abbreviation of what they intend to say. If you doubt this, just try it – read something out loud and see how it sounds; better still, record it and hear how it sounds.

- In addition, you rarely need to be able to guarantee so exact a form of wording (there are exceptions, of course; a key definition, description or numbers may need to be word perfect). It is usually more important to ensure that the emphasis, variety and pace are right and that is what is so difficult to achieve when reading.

- You need to have sufficient confidence in your knowledge that you can deliver the key ideas in a variety of ways, and not be dependent on one particular form of words. Remember that you will usually be the expert on the topic, amongst the students at least. If you forget one point, or mix up the order of things, you will still be imparting more knowledge than the other students came in with.

Preparation cannot be done in isolation. It links to two factors that are fundamental to making an effective presentation:

- purpose or objective – why exactly you are making the presentation;
- the view you take of your audience.

As many would say that the audience is the first key essential here, let us start with that.

## Your audience

Everything is easier with a clear view of your audience. First, who are they? They are likely to be in three categories:

- people you know, including fellow students;
- and also, most importantly, your lecturer or tutor;
- in some cases there may be people from outside the university in the audience.

The audience therefore includes both those who are expert and inexperienced in the topic. This presents you with a problem: what will impress your lecturers is not always the same as what will maintain the attention of your peers. Your lecturer or tutor wants you to demonstrate, through your presentation, that you have a good academic grasp of the material, that your research has been done with meticulous detail and contextualized within the wider framework of the course and programme, and that you have begun to form your own opinions and insights on the material. For them, your presentation skills are a means to an end. While a poor delivery may fail to convey your depth of preparation, a highly polished presentation lacking intellectual rigour will not impress. And impressing your lecturer or tutor is essential since they will be determining your course grades. What you should be aiming for is a well-delivered presentation demonstrating that it is based on sound research.

It is also essential to keep the attention of your fellow students, not least to ensure a productive discussion following your presentation. The technique of your presentation will be more critical here.

Specifically, any audience wants you to:

- 'know your stuff';
- look the part (in most educational establishments there is no need to dress up, but looking organized and prepared does help);
- cover the topic, theme or question provided and not digress too far from it (you will not impress your tutor if your presentation fails to reflect what they asked for);
- hold their attention and interest throughout.

It is equally important to bear in mind what audiences do not want, which includes not being:

- confused by poorly chosen language/description;
- blinded with science, technicalities or jargon;
- lost in a convoluted structure (or because there is none);
- made to listen to someone who, by being ill prepared, shows no respect for the group (or worse, for the topic).

A good presenter will always relate accurately to the theme and the audience, checking if necessary to ensure that they are doing so. The techniques explored as we move on can be used to help.

## *Clear purpose*

Rarely, if ever, will you be asked just to 'talk about' something. There will always be an angle, a question to be answered, arguments to be made or explored and contrasted. The most crucial question any intending presenter can ask themselves is simply:

Why is this presentation to be made? What are the objectives?

If you can answer that clearly, it will be easier both to prepare and present. Let us be clear here: objectives are not what you intend to say, they describe what you intend to achieve.

Apologies if this seems obvious, but many presentations fail to address the detail of their purpose: if this is to analyse a situation and draw conclusions then just talking about the facts is not going to impress. Objectives are therefore fundamental – and details about setting them are reviewed elsewhere.

## *A structure to hang things on*

Probably the most famous of all maxims about any kind of communication is the old saying 'Tell 'em, tell 'em and tell 'em'. This can be stated more clearly as meaning that you should tell people what you are going to tell them, tell them, and then tell them what it was you told them. This may sound silly, but it works – the idea is straightforward, and applies regardless of the length of the presentation.

So following this idea we will split the presentation into three sections, and look at not only how to make each effective, but how to ensure that the three together make a satisfactory whole.

# Before you speak

Having told you that there are three stages – which we review under the more businesslike headings of the beginning, the middle and the end – we are now going to discuss another factor, which is either confusing or an example of an intriguing opening! In any case, it has been referred to before – preparation. It is that which creates your beginning, middle and end and everything else along the way.

Let's unashamedly emphasize the point: preparation is important – remember Mark Twain. If he was half as good a speaker as he was a writer this makes a good point. So before we analyse a presentation, we need to think about how best to put it together.

## *Rules of preparation*

You should not start to prepare your presentation until this research or project is complete. More than likely you will end up with too much material for the presentation, and will need to be selective; this means:

- You need to select wisely. Given a short time there should be a good reason for what you decide to include, and to omit.
- Set aside additional material that may well come in handy for a future essay or exam question, and is in any case not wasted. Remember that the actual process of research will develop your academic skills.

When you have gathered all the material you need, then and only then begin to prepare the presentation. This preparation will take time, and it is as important, if not as time-consuming, as the research itself. It works best to start with main points and fill the content out – see box.

| Start with a skeleton | Add the 'flesh' | Complete the total message |
|---|---|---|
| Main point | Main point<br>Secondary point<br>Secondary point | Main point<br>• Secondary point<br>• Example/anecdote/detail<br>• Secondary point<br>• Summary |

**Action**

The first rule of preparation is always to do it; the world is full of people making lacklustre presentations and compounding the problem by saying 'I didn't have time to prepare'. Prepare systematically and doing so will get quicker and easier and more certain in terms of ensuring a crisp delivery.

## Top tips...

...for preparing to present

When you prepare:

1   Do not leave it until the last minute.

2   Do not skimp it (preparing will get quicker with practice).

3   Decide what to say (and what not to say) in light of the purpose involved.

4   Decide main points first, fill in the detail and add slides only once the overall content is clear (the systematic approach to writing, described in the last chapter, has relevance here).

5   Prepare suitable notes as an aide-mémoire to have in front of you as you speak (but not, as has been said, to read verbatim) – see box.

6   Arrange things in a logical order.

7   Think about how you will be put it over (not just the pure content, but examples, anecdotes and even an occasional appropriate element of humour).

8   Anticipate reactions and questions and plan how you will deal with these.

## Presenter's notes

Make sure that your notes are easy to interpret, legible and help you stick to time and add the emphasis required. So:

- Make the type or writing large enough to see as you stand.

- Leave some space both to allow fine-tuning and so that you can focus on things easily.

- Use symbols (consistently) to indicate repeating factors: a slide to be shown, a pause, some emphasis.

- Make main headings stand out (one way is to use two columns, with the left-hand one only containing notes of main points).

- Choose and, maybe after some experiment, stick with a format. Some people like cards. A4 sheets secured in a ring binder are manageable and stay flat (and some like to have notes and copies of slides on opposite sides of an opened folder). Choose what suits you; that's what you can work with most easily to create the impact you want.

- Always number the pages (one day you will drop them) and keep the whole thing safe and well labelled.

All this must be done with a keen eye on the required duration for the presentation so that what you prepare fits (you may need to decide the time; or you may be told the duration or have to ask what is suitable).

## A final check

A final check (perhaps after a break following preparation) is always valuable. This may also be the time to consider rehearsal, certainly if you are new to presenting: you can either talk it through to yourself, to a tape recorder or to a friend or colleague ahead of the actual event.

If you are speaking as part of a team (perhaps following a project of some sort), always make sure that those involved get together ahead of the event to rehearse, or at least discuss, both any possible overlaps and any necessary handover between speakers. You are seeking to create what appears to the audience to be a seamless transition between separate contributors.

Ultimately you need to find your own version of the procedures set out here. A systematic approach helps, but the intention is not to over-engineer the process. What matters is that you are comfortable with your chosen approach, and that it works for you. If this is the case, then, provided it remains consciously designed to achieve what is necessary, it will become a habit. It will need less thinking about, yet still act to guarantee that you turn out something that you are content meets the needs – whatever they may be.

Now consider the presentation stage by stage – start, with appropriate logic, at the beginning, and see how you can get to grips with that.

# The structure of a presentation

## Gaining attention

This is primarily achieved by your manner and by the start you make. You have to look the part; your manner has to say, 'This will be interesting. This person is prepared and knows what they are talking about.' A little has been said about such factors as appearance, standing up, and so on. Suffice it to say here that if your start appears hesitant, the wrong impression will be given and, at worst, everything thereafter will be more difficult. More important is what you say first and how it is said. The key thing is being on top of the material – confidence in presenting, and appearance, cannot make up for lack of research.

## Setting the scene

There are a number of types of opening, each presenting a range of opportunities for differing lead-ins. For example:

| A question | Rhetorical or otherwise, preferably something that people are likely to respond to positively: *Would you like to know why...?* |
|---|---|
| A quotation | This could be humorous or make a point; a classic, or novel phrase; or it might be something related to the group, for example *At the lecture on Wednesday it was said that...* |
| A story | Something that makes a point, relates to the situation or people, or draws on a common memory: *We all remember the confusion when the subject of quantum mechanics first came up...* |
| A factual statement | Perhaps striking, thought provoking, challenging or surprising: *Do you realize that more British soldiers died on the first day of the Battle of the Somme than in the Crimean and Korean Wars put together?* (The fact that this is also a question indicates that all these methods and more can be linked) |
| A dramatic statement | A story with a startling end, perhaps. Or a statement that surprises in some way |
| An historical statement | A reference back to an event that is a common experience of the group: *Last week what I said was criticized as lacking depth, so let's add some detail...* |
| A curious opening | Simply a statement sufficiently odd for people to want to find what on earth it is all about: *Consider the aardvark, and how it shares a characteristic with some of the characters in this book...* (In case you want a link, it is thick skinned) |
| A checklist | *There are 10 key stages to the process we want to discuss, first...* |

There must be more methods and combinations of methods that you can think of; whatever way you pick to start, this element of the session needs careful, and perhaps very precise, preparation.

## Creating rapport

Usually fellow students in the audience have to listen, perhaps waiting for their turn. But it is still good practice to engage them and certainly you want a tutor, perhaps saying to themselves 'I wonder what this one will be like?', to quickly change to thinking 'This sounds interesting'.

At the same time, the opening stages need to make it absolutely clear what your purpose is, what will be dealt with, and how it will be done. It must also allow you to move into the topic in a constructive way.

This opening stage is the first 'Tell 'em' from 'Tell 'em, tell 'em and tell 'em', and links to the main body of a presentation.

## The middle

The middle is the core of the presentation, and the longest segment in length. The objectives are clear:

- to put over the detail of your argument, whether you want agreement or effectively to issue a challenge or start a debate;
- to maintain attention throughout the process.

One of the principles here is to take one point at a time, and we shall do just that here.

### Putting over the content

The main trick here is to adopt a structured approach:

- Make sure you are dealing with points in a logical sequence; for instance, working through a process in a chronological order.
- Throughout, use what is referred to in communications literature (and here earlier) as 'flagging' or 'signposting', which is straight back to the three 'tell 'ems'; you cannot say things like 'There are three key points here, the problem, the research and the results; let's deal with them in turn. First, the problem...' – too much.
- Give advance warning of what is coming (this applies to both content and the nature of what is being said. Saying 'For example...' is a simple form of signposting. It makes it clear what you are doing and makes it clear also that you are not moving on to the next content point just yet.).
- Putting everything in context, and relating it to a planned sequence of delivery, keeps the message organized and improves understanding.

If this is done then the clarity it helps produce will give you the overall effect you want. People must obviously understand what you are talking about. There is no room for verbosity, for too much jargon, or for anything that clouds understanding. Your language must be precise: for example, if you aim to explain something, that explanation must be clear (nothing should start with the likes of 'It's sort of...').

## Top tips for creating understanding

Consider ensuring understanding further; nothing will be truly accepted unless this is achieved. Note that to some extent better understanding is helped by:

- Using clear, precise language – language which is familiar to those present, and which does not overuse or fail to explain jargon or specialist language.

- Making explanations clear, making no assumptions, using plenty of similes (you can hardly say 'this is like...' too often if doing so aids description), and with sufficient detail to get the point across.

- Being truly descriptive, even memorable. Consider the difference between saying something is sort of slippery or that it is as slippery as a freshly buttered ice-rink. Surely the latter phrase could not be clearer and certainly it's more memorable than the simpler alternative.

- Avoiding using phrases like 'manual excavation devices'; in presenting, a spade has to be called a spade. What is more, it has, as it were, to be an interesting and relevant spade if it is to be referred to at all and if attention is to be maintained.

## Maintaining attention

Here again the principles are straightforward. Make your presentation clear, interesting and even lively throughout. A brilliant first few minutes that tails away will quickly lose people's interest and attention.

Also make sure that the presentation remains visually interesting by using visual aids to support and enliven what you say and allow people to follow more easily.

## General principles of using visual aids

- Keep the content simple and do not read lengthy blocks of text verbatim.

- Restrict the amount of information and the number of words.

- Use single words to give structure, headings, or short statements.

- Avoid a cluttered, fussy or complicated look.

- Use a running logo (like a main heading/topic on each slide).

- Without a doubt the worst, and commonest, fault in using visual aids is to pack them so full of information (particularly dense text) as to make them more confusing than illuminating.

- Use diagrams, graphs and the like where possible rather than too many numbers; and never read figures aloud without visual support.

- Build in variety within the overall theme: for example, with colour or variations of the form of aid used.

- Emphasize the theme and structure: for example, regularly using a single aid to recap the agenda or objectives.

- Ensure that the content of the visual matches the words you will use (so, for example, do not put the word 'logistics' on a slide and then talk only about timing – it leaves people unsure quite where you are).

- Make sure that all content is necessary and relevant (a common fault is not creating original slides but using existing items – a graph or page from a paper, perhaps – and then ignoring most of what is there, focusing on only one aspect of it. People can see the rest, however, and part of their mind is distracted wondering what it is all about).

- Ensure that everything is visible, asking yourself: Is it clear? Will it work in the room? Does it suit the equipment? (Well-chosen colours and the right-sized typeface help here.)

- Ensure that the layout emphasizes the meaning you want (and not some minor detail).

- Don't add irrelevant pictures (especially Clipart); it won't improve a poor slide, it will just make it an irrelevantly illustrated poor slide.

- Pick the right aid for the right purpose.

Using any sort of visual aid needs a little orchestrating. It can be awkward initially to have to speak, keep your place, remember to show something and actually organize to do so. The answer is easy: take a moment and do not allow the process to rattle you. If people cannot see what you are doing, and frankly even if they can, just bridge any slight gap in the content of what you are saying with a descriptive comment – 'The next slide illustrates this, let me just show you'. In the time you take to say even that much, what you have to do will likely be done.

Details of the variety of ways in which you might usefully visualize things go somewhat beyond our brief, though you might check out further details in this area.

## Keeping on track

Use descriptions that incorporate stories, or anecdotes, to make the message live. You cannot make a presentation live by formal content alone; you need an occasional anecdote, or something less formal. It is nice if you are able both to proceed through the content you must present and seemingly remain flexible, apparently digressing and adding in something interesting, a point that exemplifies or makes something more interesting as you go. How do you do this? It is back to preparation; include such in your plan. Good timekeeping stems from preparation too; monitor how time is going and adjust as necessary. Remember: finishing on time is impressive.

### Action

It is helpful to include a signal about timing in your notes so that you have a regular reminder of what you intended and can check that you are on track. It may also be useful to put a watch or clock in front of you where you can see it easily (it is distracting for you and the audience to keep pulling your sleeve up to see a wristwatch).

## Questions

Questions to establish appropriate feedback may be a necessary part of this process, and in some presentations this must be done as you progress. For instance, the simplest form of this is to ask 'Is that clear?' occasionally as you go. It is also advisable to keep an eye on the visible signs, watching, for instance, for puzzled looks. Questioning technique was reviewed in Chapter 2.

Finally, continue to generate attention through your own interest and enthusiasm. After all this, when you have been through the main content, the time comes to close.

## *The end*

Always end on a high note (something that may mean that the last slide you show needs careful selection). The group expect it, if only subconsciously. It is an opportunity to build on any success during the presentation or, occasionally, to make amends for anything that has been less successful.

That apart, the end acts as a pulling together of the overall message that has been given. However you finally end, there is often a need to summarize in an orderly fashion. This is worth some thought; summarizing succinctly is not the easiest thing and thus, when well done, always impresses.

Like the beginning, there is then a need to find a way of handling the final signing off. You can, for instance, finish with:

- A question that leaves the final message hanging in the air, or makes it more likely that people will go on thinking about the issues a little longer: 'I asked a question at the start of the session, now let us finish with another...'.

- A quotation that encapsulates an important, or the last, point. A talk about presenting could perhaps close with: 'Good communication is as stimulating as black coffee, and just as hard to sleep after' (Anne Morrow Lindberg).

- Alternatively, choose something that, while not linked inextricably to the topic, just makes a good closing line.

However you decide to wrap things up, the end should be a logical conclusion, rather than something separate added to the end. If a thank you is necessary, do not make that the last thing you say. Do not say 'finally' three times and always finish on time.

# After the presentation

Two points deserve a mention here:

**1** Questions: some presentations end with a question session, in which case introduce this clearly. Certainly if you are asked (by the tutor) questions to clarify what you have said, then:

- Ensure you have the question clear before you reply (if necessary ask a question to clarify).
- You may well be able to accurately anticipate some areas of question and have a few notes that will help give a fluent reply.
- Take a moment: you can do quite a lot of thinking in the time it takes you to say 'That's a good question, let me think how best to answer it' but try to be brief.
- Never try to wing it; if you do not know say so (though you may add a comment or offer to find out).

**2** Discussion: it is perhaps more likely that there will be a group discussion after your presentation. This may be led by you or, more likely, by the tutor or lecturer. There may be specific questions or points of clarification for you, but you will not be expected to be a world expert on a subject that you have only just begun to explore. This is the moment for you to relax a little, and allow the insights of your fellow students to contribute to your learning.

All the factors mentioned here are largely common for any presentation. Different presentations do vary in importance, however. And some have more complex objectives than others: for example, some are technical and may involve demonstration.

# Post-mortem: how am I doing?

It will help accelerate your experience if you think about what you have done afterwards and aim to draw lessons from it; things to avoid, things to build on, things to use more. The checklist that follows is designed to assist this process. A manageable approach is to review matters under four headings:

- Content
- Structure
- Manner
- Maintenance of interest.

If things go well under all these headings then there is every chance something will appeal to the audience. You can mark yourself for all those factors listed and resolve if necessary to work at any areas you consider need change:

**TABLE 7.4**  Post-presentation checklist

| | Above average | Satisfactory | Below average |
|---|---|---|---|
| **Content: what you said** | | | |
| Clear and understandable<br>Level of detail<br>Level of technicality<br>Logical sequence<br>Evidence or proof<br>Link to visual aids/<br>    documentation<br>Relevance to the audience | | | |
| **Structure: arrangement of content** | | | |
| Clear objectives<br>Overall direction<br>Use of signposting<br>The Beginning: an effective<br>    start/statement of intent<br>The Middle: a logical<br>    progression<br>The End: summary/loose<br>    ends/request for action/<br>    high note<br>Continuity<br>Timing | | | |
| **Manner: impression made** | | | |
| **Maintenance of interest: appeal to audience** | | | |
| Focus on audience<br>Enthusiasm<br>Use of examples<br>Illustration<br>Humour, if appropriate<br>Visual aids: appropriate<br>    method/clear images/<br>    match what was said/<br>    illustrative<br>Management of any<br>    necessary audience<br>    involvement<br>Overall animation | | | |

If you get into the habit of coming away from everything you do and spending a moment in analysis, you will find this pays dividends in the long term.

### Action

As a final action point, make sure that you take note of how you do: after your presentations make notes of things done well (techniques to repeat) and things to avoid, change or do differently in future. Presenting is a vital skill and it is worth a moment to accelerate experience.

### Read on...

Having reviewed all the essential skills aligned directly with your study and move towards graduation, we look ahead to a time after university and at what you can do during your course to enhance your move into the world of work and make it successful.

## Your notes

..............................................................................................................

..............................................................................................................

..............................................................................................................

..............................................................................................................

..............................................................................................................

..............................................................................................................

..............................................................................................................

..............................................................................................................

..............................................................................................................

..............................................................................................................

..............................................................................................................

# 08
# The link with the world of work

**In this chapter...**

In this final chapter we look ahead to a **time after university** and how your time at university can influence your longer-term success. There are opportunities here to take action in a way that can work powerfully for you; ignoring this area can see the moment pass and put you at a disadvantage just when you want all to go well.

It was journalist Katherine Whitehorn who said: 'The best careers advice to give to the young is "Find out what you like doing best and get someone to pay you for doing it".' Would it were that easy. Realistically, moving on to the world of work can present some difficulties. As was said in the Introduction, the world of work is competitive, employers set high standards, and a qualification, however good, is rarely a passport to immediate successful selection and a job for life. The more consideration you give to the transition from study to work during your time in higher education, rather than as it ends, the easier you can make that transition and the more likely it is to go the way you want.

You may have had some experience of work as part of your course, for example on some science or business programmes you may have a year in industry, or you may have had a year working abroad as part of, say, a languages programme. On other courses, a project may have involved you working with local businesses. However, for most students their time at university is far removed from the world of work.

Two different circumstances may direct your thoughts as you look ahead; either you may:

- know what you want to do either specifically or in general terms; you may want to be a doctor, a banker or in human resources and such choices may need some refining (for example, human resources takes you so far, but into what area specifically and which sector/country do you want to work in, do you want to be with a large organization or a smaller one, a commercial one or a non-commercial one and so on are all matters that will need decision);

- not know what you want to do; in which case you will need to do some thinking during your time in higher education that aims to put you in the category above.

While it is certainly possible that over time you will change your view, not least because of experiences you have during your time at university, in either case, there are a number of areas for possible action. Just how you deal with each will depend on how far along your decision making is and what direction it is taking you in. Nothing here is complicated or likely to take very much time, but the positive difference such things can make is significant.

# Your study

Your immediate goal is to obtain the qualification you are targeting, and work – studies, projects, practical work and whatever else your course may involve – must be selected, arranged and carried out with that end in mind. But sometimes you might sensibly go further. Consider if additional work, experiences or projects might help you go beyond your coursework and assist you with the transition to the workplace that will be coming in due course. There are many and varied possibilities here. Some examples will illustrate the range:

- reading, this ranging from additional books to regular reading of a magazine or journal in a specialist area;

- research and investigation on the internet;

- meeting people or visiting organizations, ranging from a museum to an organization that might be a future employer.

**Action**

Look for opportunities and assess each possibility in this way – asking how it can help your immediate studies and how it might help beyond that. You cannot do everything and need to fit in good choices in this respect.

# Study skills: career skills

## *Social life and activities*

Life in higher education is not all work, work, work; perhaps we should say it must not be like that. You need to develop social skills and other interests, you need to relax and have fun. Many things may meet this need and add to the overall experience you are getting. Indeed, there will hopefully be time to indulge anything you fancy. If you are into athletics or astronomy then join the relevant societies or clubs; enjoy, but bear in mind that doing well at anything will look positive on your curriculum vitae (CV) later on.

Bear in mind, though, that some such activities have more direct advantages, for instance you might get involved:

- With societies and activities that have a direct bearing on your studies and extend the learning you experience in a useful way. For example, if you are studying Film, Drama, History, or a language, amongst other things, there is almost certainly a student society linked to that.

- In a capacity that produces additional experience and links to career skills as discussed above.

- In activities that link to desirable experience and skills, and you may just include things of general use or aim to link specifically with your career goals.

Note: it is worth bearing in mind how such things will appear to a prospective employer, for example involvement with something directly linked to work, and specifically work with them, will be seen as (and can be described as) good forward thinking. For example:

- Demonstrating your ability to successfully get to grips with new things promptly, for example learning a new technology. This would be impressive even if the skill itself is not particularly relevant.

- Joining a society that is relevant to your chosen career, for example membership of the Current Affairs Society if you want to be a journalist.

- Setting up a Twitter account (or the current equivalent) for your society will be seen as innovative and reflecting current cultural trends.

- Volunteering to be a music reviewer for the student magazine or a campaigner for a charity shows you are passionate about your interests. It also demonstrates personality and drive.

All this is worth some thought. It is easy to join numbers of groups early on, choosing on little more than a wave of enthusiasm or to meet or stay in contact with particular people, and then find that, while enjoyable, they serve no other useful purpose. Your choices here should certainly fit your recreational needs, but if they can do more than that then so much the more useful. This is another area where a simple pie chart might help you split and manage time spent on this sort of thing so that such activities sit comfortably alongside your work and study tasks.

---

**Action**

Choose and monitor your participation in social groups with an eye on exactly what it will involve you in and how its activities may help you, both in learning and as a relevant experience to list on your record. It may be useful to list details of the potential advantages of membership of any group you consider joining.

---

## Assessing society membership

A simple format will enable you to assess how useful memberships might be (the fun element does not need to feature here – you can assess this much less formally).

---

**Society**

Likely usefulness to your course:

'Career' skills/experience

Working as a member of a committee (or should you set your sights higher, aiming to take the chair?)

Team working

Managing people or projects

Computer work

Communications and more

---

It is worth noting points like this for a single society, or you can compare two or more as is useful; after all, time is limited and such choices matter.

## Paid work

Perhaps it is worth including paid work here too. Most students need to do some work during their time in higher education. Organizing so that the nature of the work done is useful rather than just a source of funds is not easy; it can be difficult to find suitable part-time work at all. But at least think about the nature of what you do – if you can find something with practical applications it is just one more way to get more out of the experience.

# Identifying opportunities

Be open minded, curious and enquiring about everything you are exposed to. There are many links to be made and some may not be immediately apparent. For example:

- A debating society may not rank high on your list of things to do, but if you need to develop public-speaking skills then maybe it is a good choice and something to feature on your CV later.
- Others may be more specifically linked: job applications to banks might benefit from anything linking to finance or economics and those to international organizations might similarly list any overseas involvements or trips during your course.

Particularly early on, read all the information you are given in a considered fashion to make sure you are not missing opportunities. Much like this comes through interaction with other people; hence the next heading.

# Networking

As you come to the end of your course it is worth considering who you might keep in contact with to help you in future. Obviously you will keep in touch with your close friends, but it might be worth thinking about any other people you have met on your course, in a student society or in your residence who may be a useful contact in future.

Remember that you will be moving from a familiar situation, one where most people who are useful or important are easy to maintain contact with, to one where a much wider range of disparate contacts may need to be assembled in relation to your progress into the workplace. This may well mean that a more overt and systematic approach is necessary; the following details summarize what might usefully be involved. Three things are important:

- Making contact and finding out about people. You are going to meet lots of new people and of course a major judgement is whether you like them. Will you get on? But it may be worth thinking about what they are doing, what societies they belong to, whether they would make a useful contact or collaborator. There is truth in the old saying that it is not what you know, but who you know. Both matter, of course, but do not neglect this aspect of your personal interactions – either with fellow students or others you meet along the way (including both academic and administrative staff).

- Keeping records of people: it is very easy to find yourself grasping for names – who was the guy you sat next to at some function, who said they were into computer design or whatever? Some months on, the name may escape you. It seems a bit clinical, but keep a note of anyone whom you might want to re-contact; all it takes is a simple file and a few minutes now and then – for instance a mobile phone number entered into your phone can be linked to a note in a file so that some months on you are not saying 'Who's Mary?'
- Keep in touch: it is not too difficult to maintain some sort of contact where possible collaboration may be useful. Again it may take only a few minutes and allows either party to make more specific contact later with someone who is remembered.

Having said all that, do bear in mind that classically networking is a mutual process. It works best where there are common interests (of whatever sort) and where each party can help the other. Sometimes contacts made in this way, initially without firm purpose, blossom into a really useful relationship. A factor to consider these days is that of social networking sites like Facebook. Consider creating a Facebook 'group' for your class, so that people can chat on the main forum, get in touch and swap ideas. It is also useful to create 'events' (which could just be an evening at the pub), so that you can network and get to know people who may be useful – in terms of helping you study – in the future.

**Action**

Some networking is informal and second nature – but explore what taking a slightly more formal approach can do for you. Results may soon show that this is worthwhile.

## Job seeking

There may be specific things to do here, especially as you get to the latter part of your chosen course. How to get a job (and skills like coming over well at interviews) are matters beyond our brief here, though it is worth saying that some research and thinking ahead about what's necessary is only sensible. Leaving that aside for separate study, there is one thing that needs some attention throughout your course and that concerns your CV.

As soon as you get into the process of actually applying for a job, however this is done, you will need a suitably written and logically laid out description of your experience, competencies and career intentions. At this stage note one thing about CVs: a standard one has limited use. They most often need tailoring to their purpose; so if you apply for a particular job you may sensibly reword some of your 'standard' CV to emphasize those qualities and factors that best fit you for the particular job.

When you come to it you will write a better CV if you have opened a file as you start your course and kept notes of those things that might be worth mentioning and done so progressively. The field trip you take, the committee you serve on or chair, all such things are worth noting and it will make it much easier to draft an impressive document when the time comes if you have these notes as a kind of checklist. Remember that at this stage of your life there is a limited period to document, yet there will still be a need to make a case for yourself that differentiates you from others in the eyes of a potential employer.

---

### Action

Open a CV file and keep adding to it throughout your time in higher education. You may even need to use early versions of it – to secure an industry placement as part of your course, perhaps. Doing so gives you the raw material for writing a powerful CV when it matters.

---

## Your career plan: the need for self-assessment

'If you're not planning where you want to be, what reason do you have for worrying about being nowhere?' So said business guru Tom Hopkins and it is a fair point. Whatever you may want or intend doing this makes sense and, as was said earlier, if you do not take steps to make a decision you may be left nowhere. Make sure you use your university's Careers Service, especially if you are uncertain as to the career you wish to follow. Don't think that you need to know exactly what you want to do when you leave before you can visit; the opposite is true. The Careers Service can help you:

- get to know the wide range of careers and employers available;
- identify the career options available to individuals with your (future) qualification;
- work through your own ideas, and identify the best career options for you;

- prepare for the career you wish to follow, identifying the skills and expertise you will need, or any further training necessary;
- secure a placement as a kind of test drive, and to obtain work experience;
- maximize your chances of securing a job in your chosen field.

Making contact with the Careers Service early in your course will ensure that you get maximum benefit. In any case, towards the end of your course you are likely to need an immediate focus on examinations.

If you are to influence your career, certainly if you are to positively influence it, then you need to be clear about the direction in which you want it to go. This may sound obvious and easy, but in fact implies a good deal and needs some careful thought. When one of us (PF) was at school he wanted to be an astronomer. This was born of a passionate interest in the subject rather than any link with actual or likely abilities, but it was still his earliest career plan. However, on checking out what might be necessary, realism soon set in and, though the interest continues, career progress took other paths. Career planning, perhaps sadly, does not mean just conjuring up plans that are no more than pie in the sky. Aim high by all means, but proceed also on a clear, accurate and honest assessment of what might realistically be possible.

## Action

Deciding the direction you want to take must first involve some inward analysis. Again this is activity that can usefully take place during rather than after your course, not least because you want to minimize the time between your course finishing and starting a job. Spend a moment, go about it the right way and it can pay dividends.

We doubtless all like to think we know ourselves, but this may not be entirely true. It is easy to make assumptions, to leave key elements out of the picture and so, as a result, misjudge how our current profile lends itself to career progress, and just what sort of progress may be possible. Assumptions can link back to past experience, fears, bad experiences or a host of things.

The first step to deciding a route forward from your current position is to look at where you are at the moment (or where you hope to be once you have your qualification). This should be done systematically and honestly and you may find it useful to keep some notes of what the thinking produces. The next several sections lead you through a suitable and proven progression of self-analysis, which assesses your skills, work values, personal characteristics, and also your non-work characteristics. Of course, let's say up front that your view of some of these things may change. So be it, but you have to start somewhere and can always adapt your view over time.

# Self-assessment

Areas for review are your:

- skills;
- work values;
- personal characteristics;
- non-work characteristics.

These are now addressed in turn; if you are just starting your course do not worry that you may not be able to produce a definitive list under each heading, but importantly do note that by the time you approach the end of your time at university you need to be able to make a good shot at this or it will be difficult to direct your job-seeking activities or know what you want to achieve.

## *Assess your skills*

You might be surprised at how many skills you have. Remember that it is quite possible that things you do and take for granted, you can only in fact do because of some experience. Tick off the following skills that you have learnt and consider how you can transfer them to your CV. For example, if you feel you have mastered the art of presentations, on your CV you can confidently write that you have 'excellent communication skills,' and be able to provide an example.

---

**Action**

Make notes to link your growing list of experience and skills to your record as it will be seen by prospective employers on your CV. Thus do not just say 'I belonged to the XYZ Society'. Say 'I gained experience of communications and team working by being an active member of the XYZ Society, chairing their ABC Committee and organizing projects such as...'. This sort of thing can add powerfully to your profile at a key time.

| Skill | Link to work |
|---|---|
| Essay writing | • Report writing<br>• Writing business documents<br>• Research skills<br>• Creative thinking |
| Presentation skills | • Communication skills<br>• Negotiating skills<br>• Presenting business proposals |
| Time management | • Able to work to deadlines<br>• Project management skills<br>• Organization |
| Team working | • Leadership<br>• Able to take instructions<br>• Communications |
| Use of appropriate technologies | • Computer literate<br>• Knowledge of social networking sites (for marketing roles)<br>• E-communications |

The format that follows will give you basis to create a personal version of this, as in the example using one of the categories mentioned above. This can go into whatever detail is appropriate, for example under computer literacy you might want to list specific software programs with which you are familiar.

| **Presentation skills** | Persuading |
|---|---|
|  | Negotiating |
|  | Promoting ideas |
|  |  |
|  |  |
|  |  |

| Main skills categories | Subsidiary skills |
|---|---|
| | |
| | |
| | |
| | |
| | |
| | |
| | |
| | |
| | |
| | |

Even before your work career really starts you should have the full picture in mind and recorded. Bear in mind too that:

- such a list will change over time;
- you may see gaps or omissions in such a list; these you can resolve to fill in terms of adding or extending competencies.

Decide which headings along the lines of the above are right for you, and make some notes. It might be an interesting exercise to do this now while this book is focusing your mind on it, then checking and revising it occasionally as your time in higher education progresses. Some of the topics listed above will recur as headings in their own right and you may view things differently after a review of how important some of the skill areas are from a career point of view.

## Assess your work values

It is not enough to know what skills you have. These must be viewed along-side your work values. For instance, ask if you have:

- a strong need to achieve;
- a need for high financial reward;
- high work interest/satisfaction requirements;
- a liking for doing something 'worthwhile';
- a desire to do something creative;
- specific requirements (such as to travel, to be independent, innovative or part of a team).

A wide range of permutations may be involved here (think about it) and such may change over time. For example, travel may be attractive to the young and single but less so to people who have young children, and then it may become more attractive again when a family is older.

## Assess your personal characteristics

Most people do not change their habits and ways, at least they do not do so dramatically and certainly not without effort, once they are old enough to be into a career. You need to assess yourself in this respect and do so honestly. Ask for example:

- Are you innovative?
- Positive?
- Optimistic?
- Hard working?
- Prepared to take risks?
- What sort of a person, in fact, are you?

Again a simple format will allow you to record any self-analysis you do here.

### Personal characteristics

There may be a clash here. In thinking through your work values you feel that you may be suited to, and want to be involved in, something with considerable cut and thrust, that is innovative, creative and which generally puts you working at the leading edge. However, an honest assessment of yourself may show that, whatever the superficial or status attraction of this option, it is just not really you. For example, risk taking may not be your thing and a different, perhaps more supportive role may seem to be where you are likely to excel most. Again list what you feel is relevant about yourself here.

## Assess your non-work characteristics

Realistically, work and social life have to coexist alongside each other. They may do so peaceably, or there may be conflicts between them. It is not automatically necessary to career success to be a workaholic, though a strictly 9 to 5 attitude to the job is perhaps not recommended (or possible) either. And on the positive side, work and interests or hobbies may overlap constructively, the one teaching you something about the other. There will be questions to be asked here too:

- What are your family/social circumstances?
- Where do you need/want to live?
- How much time can you spend away from home?
- What are your other responsibilities and interests?

Consider family and interests specifically:

- Family: If you have good friends, a partner, wife or husband then priorities may need to be set, because career-building priorities can clash. It is, sadly, perfectly possible to arrive successfully at the top of the heap – a success in career terms, but with home, social life and happiness in ruins. This may sound dramatic, but the issues here are worth some serious thought. Not least, there are times when career decisions must be made fast or opportunities will be lost. If the relationships between home, family and work have never been discussed, then the person who comes home from the office to tell their partner 'I have this great new opportunity with the company, but it means living in Hong Kong for two years' is in for some heated debate, especially if they have promised to go back to the office the next day with a decision. Such situations can occur at every stage of a career. They are not dependent on which half of a partnership instigates them and are made more complicated by changing and more complex circumstances as you get older.
- Interests: Interests are an important issue. All work and no play is, for most of us, a bad thing. You need to look at your interests and hobbies alongside the job and your future career intentions. Can they move forward together? How much time do you want to put into hobbies, social life and work? These are not easy questions and must be worked

out over a period of time. Even so, there may come times when there are clashes; especially with things that have wide impact such as working overseas. If you have thought it all through, and discussed it with other family members as appropriate, then transient problems are more likely to be just that – transient.

Once you have completed this personal analysis it then needs to be related to the outside world.

# Linking your analysis of yourself with market demands

Whatever profile your various self-analysis exercises builds up, it must match realistically with the demands made by employers in the marketplace. Let's put that more specifically: it must match up with the demands made by employers in whatever sector you intend to excel in. So, while there are perhaps generally desirable characteristics that we might list, being:

- adaptable to change (or able to prompt it);
- flexible;
- self-sufficient;
- thorough;
- productive and so on;

... there will be more specific characteristics in terms of abilities and nature which will be demanded in a particular field. Indeed, a certain competence or characteristic may be an asset in one area and frowned on in another, as something like creativity might be differently regarded in an advertising agency and a more traditional business. Similarly, what for some is drive and initiative might be regarded elsewhere as aggressive and self-seeking.

Consider the implications of this: having analysed yourself and your intended field of employment, then, if the analysis does not persuade you that mismatching must make you look elsewhere, you must aim to cultivate the appropriate profile for success in that field. The better the match, the better the chances are that your profile will allow you to do well, and progress along your chosen path.

Success is not, however, guaranteed simply by a good match. An anecdote will perhaps illustrate a point arising from this fact. A good friend had a son who had just left acting college and was intent on carving out a career on the stage. We went to see a play he was in at a small London 'fringe' theatre; a production in which the cast were all young people starting out on their careers. His performance – as Macbeth – seemed excellent, and this was expressed to the friend later. 'What else did you notice?' he asked and, when no answer came, he commented, 'Everyone in the cast was excellent'. His point was that talent was not going to be the only factor in his son's possible success. He is good, but he has to get ahead of a strong field just to work regularly in this field, and certainly to rise to the rank of star. So it is in many fields. Just having the right qualifications and aptitudes is rarely sufficient – others have them too – you have to have them in the right amount and at the right level; and they must show. Then if you work at it (and perhaps have some good luck too, though this is not something to rely on), you may carve out success for yourself. But never make the mistake of thinking this happens in a vacuum – it happens with others around you trying to do similar things. The workplace is inherently competitive. Knowing how well you match up is, nevertheless, a good starting point – one worth some thought.

## Sum up your analysis and set clear goals

As management guru Peter Drucker said in a much-copied phrase about businesses, 'If you do not know where you are going, any road will do.' It is true; you need a plan and having one does make a difference. As with any business – so it is with any career. It's surely no more than common sense, and yet conversely it is so very easy to wake up one day and find that what we have been wont to regard as planning is actually wholly insubstantial. Having said that objectives are important, another point should be made: they must be flexible. Life in all its aspects, certainly within organizations which might employ you, is dynamic. Objectives cannot be allowed to act as a straight-jacket, yet we need their guidance, so their potential for acting to fix things should not be regarded as a reason not to have them.

In the business world, people talk of 'rolling' plans. By this is meant a plan that is reasonably clear and comprehensive for the shorter term, then sets out broad guidelines and further ahead has only main elements clearly stated. As time goes by, the plan can be updated and advanced into the future. With your career in mind, you will find a similar approach works well. In the short term, when you can anticipate more of what may happen, the detail of how you intend to proceed is clearer; further ahead you have notes on the outline strategy and key issues. For instance, remembering to decide that 'My objective is to become a marketing director' is not much help without some clear actions and steps along the way.

## Clear information

Some research may be useful alongside all this. For example, you may, as was said, want work in business and (ultimately) be a marketing director. But do you know what that entails? Really? Check it out. The box shows a typical job description for the post of marketing manager, a step below the board-level job.

---

### Marketing Manager

Description

Responsible for the strategic direction of all marketing activity on specific products/services

Personal specification

3+ years experience in marketing – or product management

Able to think strategically and direct delivery

Works well in multi-disciplined teams

Forms close-knit relationships with outside agencies

Responsibilities

Reports to Marketing Director

Ensures product/service matches brand positioning

Identifies target markets and works with data manager to provide external agencies with relevant data

Plans communication strategy and liaises with all members of the campaign team to ensure effective and efficient delivery

Analyses results of all marketing activity and presents findings and recommendations to senior management/product management

Builds close-knit teams, own and cross-departmental

Liaises with external agencies to ensure clear understanding of the marketing strategy.

---

The above is probably the sort of description that would best fit a largish company, maybe in the consumer products area (where external advertising agencies are often used). Whatever interests you, some checking may be useful; here a body like the Chartered Institute of Marketing might provide useful information. You need to think about sources too. Such a picture can usefully be linked to the skills such a job demands. To continue the example, as well as knowledge and experience of marketing, such a person needs to:

● be an effective manager (able to recruit, select, train, plan, organize, and control a diverse group of people);

- take a long-term view (ie direct the business, set strategic objectives and define a framework of targets, priorities and policies to drive towards them);
- understand and be able to work with other business functions as necessary (eg production and finance);
- be numerate (because marketing is concerned with profit generation);
- know and be able to utilize new and IT technology as necessary;
- be productive (time management is important in every job);
- make effective decisions;
- communicate effectively;
- remain close to the market and understand customers;
- achieve results, not just organize activities.

It is clearly beyond possibilities to analyse even this one job in more detail, let alone every job that might interest you, in the space available. But the principle is clear. You need to make sure you know sufficient about the field you aim for and base what you do on this knowledge.

## Making objectives useful

Objectives should be SMART. This well-known mnemonic stands for specific, measurable, achievable, realistic and timed, thus:

Specific – expressed clearly and precisely.

Measurable – it must be possible to tell if you have achieved something (the difference between saying you want to be 'very successful' or to be 'marketing director').

Achievable – what you aim for must not be so difficult as to be pie in the sky; otherwise the plan that goes with it similarly becomes invalid and of no practical help in taking things forward.

Realistic – it must fit with your self-analysis and be what you want; it might be a valid objective to aim for something possible but not ideal (promotion might be possible within a department, but your real intention is to get out beyond that) but this will not be helpful. Action is needed with more ambitious objectives in mind.

Timed – this is important; objectives are not to be achieved 'eventually' but by a particular moment: when do you aim to be marketing director, this year, next year or when?

There is no need for you to complete elaborate documentation here. Any objectives and any plans are purely for your own guidance, but a few notes on paper may be useful and there are times (such as when your spell of higher education is finishing) when it may be useful to think of current events alongside the notes you have made. If you not only know which road you should be on, but have taken steps to make sure you go purposively along it, then that is a good start. It certainly helps answer the first two important questions, the answers to which help direct your career: Do you know what you want? And, are you aiming high?

If you have never thought things through before in this kind of way, then we recommend doing so to you. It may take a moment initially, but once done needs little time to keep updated. If you always base all your career choice, career management and development activity on such sound analysis, clear thinking and specific objectives then it is more likely that both your long-term action and the way you spot and take advantage of opportunities along the way will take you where you want to go.

## Research to assist your progress

There is an important point to accept here, and it is one reinforced by the old saying that 'information is power'. Your career plan can only succeed if it is based on fact. So, you may need to know such things as:

- what prevailing salary levels are in a particular function or industry;
- how many companies operate in a certain field or are located in a particular town;
- or, what qualifications are normally essential entry requirements in your kind of job in, say, Australia.

Whatever it is, you should check, check carefully and, if necessary, check again. Sources have never been more prolific. If it needs a telephone call, a visit to a good library or an hour on the internet, so be it. It is your life and career and it is surely too important to base on hunch, hearsay or out-of-date information.

### Action

Listing the many possible sources that might be relevant to research to assist a career plan is beyond the space and brief here, but some, when you have discovered them, should be noted carefully; you may well need them again.

# An action plan

Certainly towards the end of your course, these thoughts should take on the form of an action plan. This may well be a plan that you show to no one else. It does not need to be written up like a report, indeed it may be brief, but you should have a record of certain things in writing. Keep this safely, perhaps with other related documents and information (for example, your draft CV).

**TABLE 8.4**  Action plan

| Goal | Achieve this by... | What I need to do to get there | How do I do this? |
|---|---|---|---|
| eg be a French teacher | eg 2013 | eg do work experience at the local school | eg write my CV and send to the local school |
|  |  |  |  |
|  |  |  |  |
|  |  |  |  |
|  |  |  |  |
|  |  |  |  |
|  |  |  |  |

In addition, it may also be worth listing thoughts requiring more work to realize them – 'I must find a way to get an opportunity to travel' – and then amending these into more specific objectives.

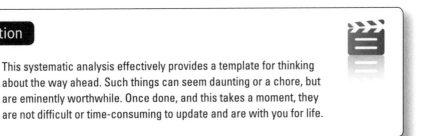

**Action**

This systematic analysis effectively provides a template for thinking about the way ahead. Such things can seem daunting or a chore, but are eminently worthwhile. Once done, and this takes a moment, they are not difficult or time-consuming to update and are with you for life.

As you move on from your time in higher education you want to have gained as much as possible, in every way possible, from the experience. As this chapter illustrates, maximizing the experience is not something that 'just happens'. Rather it needs some thought and it needs working at. Doing both is certainly worthwhile. And, though it is obvious enough, remember that it is too late as you leave college or university to be realizing that a little more thought or a greater involvement in something during your time there would have given you a better overall experience and a better stepping stone into the world of work.

Some of the thoughts expressed in this chapter may seem to look too far ahead; perhaps too far ahead to worry about. But you know what the speed of change is like, you know, from these pages not least, that the workplace is competitive and you will have heard the phrase lifelong learning (and be aware, too, how some careers demand what is called Continuous Professional Development (CPD) to ensure that those working in them keep up to date). So it makes sense to regard a little thought and action ahead of time as something that can make things easier and more certain; forewarned is forearmed. The appendix to this chapter sets out the key approaches necessary once you start the job-seeking process in earnest.

# APPENDIX TO CHAPTER 8:
## Top tips for effective job seeking

This is a task to be approached carefully and more information about the process may well be necessary; however, here are some top tips. It is a pre-requisite of successful job seeking to:

- Prepare a first class CV: There is no such thing as a standard CV. It will need amending to produce the emphasis appropriate to an application for a particular job, and may also need to vary depending for instance on the industry in which the job exists, the size of the organization, its location and, not least, the precise configuration of the job and the skills and experience required.

- Compose a first-class individual covering letter: while a CV can be a true reflection of someone's abilities, many are the result of advice and some are written by someone other than the applicant (eg an agency). Employers know this, so in a small, but significant, way the content and tone of a letter can add to the information that is weighed in the balance to decide whether an applicant goes forward to interview stage. The letter needs to explain the following:

  - why you are sending out your CV;
  - significant things about your background and skills;
  - the sort of person you are;
  - the special contribution you can offer;
  - what you would like to happen next;
  - how you can be contacted.

  For more information on cover letters, see *Preparing the Perfect Job Application*, by Rebecca Corfield (published by Kogan Page).

- Be realistic: employers use a variety of criteria to make the recruitment process manageable. It is said that the ideal recruitment advertisement prompts one reply – from a candidate who is both suitable and appointed. Requests for candidates are designed to focus the process, securing a smaller number of applicants from those who are exclusively 'on spec'. So be realistic. Apply for jobs that are stretching your credentials a little by all means but do not hide the fact that you are somewhat off-spec (if you are); it will be seen anyway. Explain why, despite this, you feel you should be considered.

- Research the employer organization: if – when! – you move to the next stage, you really must not go into an interview and ask what the company does. Employers like it if an interest has clearly been taken (get their annual report, check their website and the press, send for a brochure) and the information you discover can help you decide what kind of things to raise at an interview.

- Prepare for the interview: in the sense of both checking out good interview practice and preparing for each one. The latter means thinking through: what you might be asked; what you should ask; making some notes and aiming to create a link between your experience and credentials and the job itself.

- Be yourself: there is a danger that all this care and preparation may come over as a stilted approach. Employers want to know about you, the real you. Of course, you want to paint a full picture and leave out nothing that might weigh in the balance in your favour, but for all the checking of details, the way you present yourself counts for a good deal too.

- Be honest: there is research which suggests that almost a quarter of applicants lie on job application forms, and then presumably at interview. Resist the temptation to say you were studying for a postgraduate degree when you spent the time selling shell necklaces on a beach in Goa. It should not be surprising that many employers check, indeed this may be most likely amongst those you would consider the most desirable sort of employer.

For more information go to **www.koganpage.com/resources/ PreparingThePerfectCV** (password: CV1347) and **www.koganpage.com/ resources/PreparingThePerfectJobApplication** (password: JA4347) where you can access downloadable template CVs and cover letters.

Note: you do not want to lose opportunities for want of information, so when you get to the job-seeking stage you may want to check exactly how it is best to make such approaches.

## Read on...

There is little more to say. If you have read right through this book then you have had an opportunity to review the essential approaches necessary to university success. Of course, all courses vary to some extent, but you will doubtless need to work hard and in a way that suits the course – and these essentials are not only likely to assist you do that and make life a little easier, but also make success a little more certain. The one factor that is always involved is you – a thought we turn to briefly next for a final word.

# Your notes

# 09
# **And finally...**

**N**ow a final thought reflecting everything written earlier. Right now, if you are at the beginning of your studies, you are in a strong position and face a significant opportunity. The time ahead may well be demanding and some hard work is assuredly going to be necessary, but you have the opportunity to maximize its effectiveness. Deploying the right approaches, and taking steps so that you can do so – studying, considering, trying and fine-tuning what needs to be done – can make the course you take smoother and the likelihood of a good degree classification surer. If you are already further through your course as you read this, then such action may need taking more urgently.

The fact is that, as this text has aimed to make clear, you need to:

- manage your time well;
- go about your studies in the right way;
- develop your independent and critical thinking;
- exercise self-motivation and self-discipline;
- take on board skills such as writing and presenting;
- work with the various academic and other staff in your place of learning;
- utilize the various processes and systems involved in a considered and practical fashion.

Just how well you do all this will directly affect the outcome of your degree; but there is nothing that has been reviewed here that is beyond the determined and motivated student. There is not so much recommended that it cannot be manageably integrated into your life and work. The danger is twofold: first, that you underestimate the need for all this (the 'I can wing it' approach) and therefore never actually set out to work in this sort of way to the degree that will help; secondly, that you leave serious consideration too late – then whatever you do and however seriously you may take it, you risk not catching up and failing, at worst perhaps by a small margin.

Logically, most people accept that further education is a great opportunity, that it needs to be worked at and that doing so needs a new skills armoury if progress is going to be smooth and not unnecessarily complicated. Yet not everyone succeeds. Of course, some people fail because their chosen subject defeats them. So be it. There may be nothing some could do to avoid this. But how much worse to fail and know that you could have succeeded: the classic 'If only...' situation. The rewards of a considered approach are huge, not just to the outcome of your degree, but also to the way in which this whole period of your life will go. You want it to be interesting, enjoyable, satisfying and fun, and there is no intention here to suggest that you should not find it so: indeed, the approaches described here make establishing a balance between the various aspects of student life, so that it is all enjoyable, smoother and thus more likely to be made to happen.

Graduation is not a destination. It's a stepping stone. Making sure you get there, and then on to wherever it may take you, are both down to you. You will be better able to succeed if you are well informed and take a little time to go about things in the most effective way. You need to insist to yourself that certain things are priorities. As John Adams, the second president of the United States, said: 'We cannot guarantee success, but we can deserve it.' Finally, remember that while luck can play a part, good luck is not to be relied on as a panacea. Thus it is logical to end not by wishing you luck, but rather, just as was done in the Foreword, by wishing you well.

# Your notes

.................................................................................................

.................................................................................................

.................................................................................................

.................................................................................................

.................................................................................................

.................................................................................................

.................................................................................................

.................................................................................................

.................................................................................................

.................................................................................................

.................................................................................................

.................................................................................................

.................................................................................................

# APPENDIX
# The student/university relationship

A recurring theme through this book has been seeking and obtaining assistance along the way from wherever it may be available. Universities are conscious of student requirements and many different kinds of assistance are available in most of them, many referred to here. Students have a right to expect their university to support them, but it is a two-way process and students have responsibilities too.

Many universities communicate about the various processes and responsibilities involved and as a final part of this book it seems worth quoting one such message in full. The text that follows is the *Student Charter of Anglia Ruskin University*, which operates in Cambridge and Chelmsford. It was selected because it seems to the authors to be an excellent example of such a document – and we are pleased to thank Anglia Ruskin for their permission to reproduce it here.

Whichever university you attend it will probably issue similar information. Seek it out and be sure to read it; such can set the scene for a satisfactory working arrangement with your chosen institution.

## Introduction

This student charter aims to explain, in language which is easy to understand, exactly what you can expect of us and, in return, what we expect of you. It is set out to show a student's experience – from applying to us to graduating and becoming a life-member, or 'alumnus', of the Anglia Ruskin community.

While you are a student at Anglia Ruskin University, we expect that you will:

- respect the people you meet and learn to work well with other students and staff;
- take an active part in, and contribute to, your learning and become involved in as many areas of university life as possible;
- respect, and keep to, our values; and
- not do anything to damage our reputation.

In return you can expect all members of our university to treat you with respect.

An important part of being a student is giving feedback on your experience of university life. We will give you opportunities to do this and we will use your feedback to help us make improvements. If you are an undergraduate student you will be able to take part in the National Student Survey in your final year, and we very much hope that you will do so.

Finally, if you are a full-time student:

- you will need to study for at least 35 hours each week; and
- you should not normally do more than 15 hours of paid work each week.

Research shows that success as a student is best achieved when you get the right balance of study and work.

All the commitments in this charter apply to you if you are studying at one of our main sites – Chelmsford, East Road, Cambridge, Fulbourn and Peterborough (hospital). In this charter, 'we' means the Anglia Ruskin University Higher Education Corporation, and 'you' means a student who is registered and studying at one of Anglia Ruskin University's campuses. We are working on a charter that will apply to our students who are registered at a joint-venture centre, or who are studying through 'distance learning' or through one of our partner colleges or organisations.

We divide our teaching times into semesters because most of our students study on this pattern. If you would like us to give you our teaching times in a different format, please ask us.

# Before you arrive

## 1. When you apply

We will:

- consider all applications fairly and offer places to people who will get the greatest benefit from our courses;
- publish a prospectus that contains accurate, relevant information about courses, conditions for admission, the availability of accommodation, local childcare facilities, support services, and costs;
- make sure that our application process meets the needs of people with disabilities and that all our staff are aware of such needs;
- give applicants information about open days and other events they might want to go to. We will do this at least 20 working days before the event. If the event is within this period, we will send the information immediately.

We expect you to:

- give us complete, honest and accurate information in your application;

- give us any supporting work or evidence we ask for straightaway, so that we can give you a prompt decision on your application;
- come for an interview (if we ask you to);
- tell us about any disability, learning difficulty, personal circumstance or an illness you have that may affect your learning at Anglia Ruskin (so we can make any adjustments we need to make); and
- find out as much as you can about what we can offer you, for example by coming to one of our open days or visiting our website.

## 2. If we offer you a place

We will:

- make a decision on your application once we have all the information we need and, if you are successful, send you our offer and any conditions attached to it within 15 working days;
- send you, with our offer, information on how to apply for a place in university accommodation; and
- respond to your application for university accommodation within 10 working days of receiving it.

We expect you to:

- reply to our offer by the given deadline; and
- apply to rent university accommodation within two weeks of accepting our offer (if you want to rent university accommodation).

## 3. Tuition fees and money

We will:

- publish our tuition fees on our website at least six months before the start of your course and every year after that;
- help you to understand our tuition fees, scholarships and bursaries and any other financial help you may be able to get (we will reply to your question within three working days and we aim to give you a full response within 13 working days); and
- use the student complaints procedure to sort out any problems between us and you about fees and other financial matters.

We expect you to:

- make all the necessary arrangements with whoever is paying your tuition fees (such as your employer or a local authority), before your course starts;

- pay your tuition fees when they are due (if you are personally responsible for paying them); and

- tell us if you will find it difficult to continue with any agreement you have made with us about paying your tuition fees. You must do this before the fees are due.

## 4. If you accept our offer

We will:

- send you information about how we will welcome you within 10 working days of receiving your acceptance;

- give you access to our student guide on the internet;

- if you are from outside the UK, we will send you our Guide for International Applicants and invite you to a special orientation programme before the beginning of your first semester; and

- send you clear instructions about where and when to arrive. You should receive these within 10 working days before you are due to start. If you are due to start within 10 working days we will send them straightaway.

We expect you to:

- read any information we send you before you arrive; and

- visit our website to find out more about what will happen when you arrive

# When you arrive

## The first few days

We will:

- help you to register for your course within the first three days of our welcome period (we are introducing online registration from 2008 and if you can register online we will send you details of how to do so);

- give you our student handbook, our assessment regulations and our rules, regulations and procedures for students;

- give you your username and password for our computer facilities, no more than 24 hours after you have registered (you will be able to see your account details on E-Vision, our student-information service on the internet);

- tell you who your personal tutor is (your personal tutor will arrange to meet you during the first four weeks of your course); and

- organise a programme of events to help you meet other students during your first few days as a new student.

We expect you to:

- arrive at the time we asked you to arrive – or tell us if you are going to be late;
- register for your course, either online before you arrive or at the time we tell you;
- make sure that you have received our student handbook, our assessment regulations and our rules, regulations and procedures for students, and keep them to refer to in the future;
- meet your personal tutor at the arranged time; and
- take part in the programme of events to show that you want to get involved in university life.

# When your course starts

## 1. Learning and teaching

We will:

- give you information on our website about the timetable in general (we will tell you about the availability of modules, and class times six teaching weeks before the class begins);
- give you access to your personal timetable six weeks before the start of the first semester and at least two weeks before the start of the second semester;
- give you access to your personal timetable on E-vision three working days after you have registered online (if you are a new student);
- tell you if the time or location of a class is going to be changed (we will normally do this by 9am of the morning of the class);
- monitor your attendance at timetabled classes and contact you if you do not go often enough to class;
- aim to rearrange, as soon as possible, any class we have to cancel;
- reply to any problem or question about your course within three working days and aim to give you a full response within 13 working days;
- give you a module guide – information about day-to-day studies on each of your modules – no later than the beginning of your module (the module guide may be available on our website);
- offer a drop-in or appointment service where you can speak to academic staff (they will be available for at least three hours each week); and
- tell you what support is available to help you in your studies.

We expect you to:

- have the information you need about your course and your timetable;
- follow the advice in your module guide about what you need to study as you work through the semester;
- go to your classes on time;
- take an active part in all your classes;
- tell us as soon as possible of any problems that may affect your work or your progress;
- go to all off-campus activities that are part of your course; and
- follow any advice we give you to help you in your studies.

## 2. Assessing your work

We will:

- give you, at the beginning of the module, all the information you need about assessment, including the deadline, the format your assignment should be in and the marking scheme;
- give you clear advice about what you must not do, such as trying to pass off someone else's work as your own (plagiarism);
- tell you when and where to hand in your assignment and what happens if you hand it in late – written assignments are normally handed in to, and collected from, i-centres (student information centres);
- give you a receipt when you hand in your assignment to the i-centres;
- publish, on our exams website, a detailed examination timetable at least four weeks before the first examination;
- offer extra academic support if you have to 'resit' an examination (take it again) or if you have to do an assignment again;
- publish, on our exams website, a detailed 'resit' examination timetable at least 10 working days before the first 'resit' examination;
- give you feedback on your assignments within 20 working days, or 30 working days in the case of your major project; and
- discuss your exam script (answers) with you if you ask us to.

We expect you to:

- make sure that you have received and understood all the relevant information about assessment, including deadlines, exam dates and how you should present your assignment;
- be aware of the academic rules relating to your studies (we will give you a short version of the rules, called the 'assessment regulations', when you first register);

- take part in all the activities you will be assessed in, and, in particular, turn up for your examinations at the time and place shown in the examination timetable;

- present your written work in a word-processed format, and include all appropriate references;

- hand in your assignments by the set deadline;

- keep receipts for your assignments until you receive marked copies back;

- keep copies or electronic back-ups of your written work, until you receive marked copies back;

- collect your marked assignments and keep them until you finish your course (we cannot give you your exam scripts back, but we can discuss them with you);

- take note of feedback on your work and try to learn from it to help you improve in future assessments; and

- tell us of any special needs you have or of any circumstances that may affect how you prepare, present or hand in your assignments.

## 3. How we will handle difficulties

We have three procedures to help us deal with any problems.

- The student complaints procedure – you should use this procedure if you want to make a formal complaint because you believe we have not kept our promises to you.

- The appeals procedure – you should use this procedure to appeal against an academic decision (for example, if you don't agree with how we have handled your assessment).

- The student discipline procedure – we will use this procedure if we have to take action against you because we believe that you have broken the code of conduct.

For all three procedures, we will:

- give you a copy of our rules, regulations and procedures for students, which contains information about each procedure and a copy of our code of conduct for students;

- keep to the deadlines in each procedure;

- be fair and reasonable at all times;

- not treat you differently from other students because you have been involved in any procedure;

- help you to understand how the procedures work and encourage you to ask for help from the Students' Union; and

- keep a record of the number of times each procedure is used and how each case was dealt with, to help us improve the procedures.

For all three procedures, we expect you to:

- be fair and reasonable if you are involved in any procedure;
- follow the procedure closely, provide supporting evidence and keep records of all relevant facts; and
- keep to the deadlines in any procedure.

In line with the student complaints procedure, we will:

- be happy to discuss any concerns you have before you make a formal complaint;
- investigate your concern or complaint fully and fairly;
- respond to you appropriately and politely, explaining how we have carried out our investigation; and
- take prompt and effective action to sort any problem out.

In line with the student complaints procedure, we expect you to:

- try to sort out any problems with the person who is directly involved, with another member of staff or with the Students' Union advice service (this can help to stop the problem becoming a formal complaint);
- be reasonable in your response to any action we take to solve the problem; and
- use the student complaints procedure fully before trying to involve any outside organisations.

In line with the student discipline procedure, we expect you to:

- be aware of the university's rules, regulations and procedures for students and our code of conduct for students;
- behave respectfully to our staff, students, visitors and neighbours at all times; and
- respond reasonably to any informal warning about behaviour that breaks the code of conduct.

# How we will support you

## 1. The university library

We will:

- enrol you as a member of the library when you register as a student with us;

- offer extensive opening hours at our major sites during the academic year (the opening hours depend on which site you use);
- provide access to online services and resources at all times, with a maximum of 5% downtime (time when resources may not be available because we have to carry out maintenance) in any year;
- have staff available to help you in person, by e-mail, online and by phone, at major sites during the academic year;
- have in stock at least one copy of every item on your recommended-reading list;
- make items that have been returned available within two hours of them being returned (when library staff are on duty);
- provide an inter-library loan service (this allows us to borrow UK publications from other libraries if we don't have them in stock) and supply 85% of articles within seven working days, and 85% of books within 14 working days;
- maintain our equipment and facilities in good working order, with at least 90% of machines working at any time; and
- make you aware of new services and improvements, and changes in the availability of services (we will give you at least seven days' notice if any service will not be available).

To help us provide the best possible service, we expect you to:

- consider the needs and rights of other library users;
- use the different areas of the library for the purpose they are meant for;
- keep your workspace reasonably tidy;
- treat library staff with respect, keep to the rules, policies and procedures, and use the facilities appropriately;
- get to know your way around the library, the main features of the website and digital library, and the basic services and procedures;
- take advantage of sessions we provide to help you use the library – they will help you develop as an independent learner;
- check your university e-mail account regularly for library notices; and
- let us know if you have any problems with the library service.

## 2. How we will communicate with you

We will give you:

- a student e-mail account with 200MB of storage space;
- online access to information, such as your timetable, exam timetable, and results, using E-vision;

- 20MB of storage on the university's central network so you can save documents and files (you will have access to the central network from any computer, on or off campus); and

- online training in how to use your student e-mail account and E-vision.

We expect you to:

- follow the training instructions for using your student e-mail and E-vision, and ask for help if you have any problems;

- check your student e-mail inbox at least twice a week, as this will be our main method of communicating with you;

- check your personal details on E-vision to make sure that they are correct and up to date and tell us of any changes;

- use the communications system responsibly and do nothing that might damage our reputation; and

- report any fault or problem, using your Anglia Ruskin University e-mail address, as soon as you can and give us as much detail as possible so we can help to sort it out.

## 3. Support for students from outside the UK

We will:

- give you full and accurate information about the UK and about Anglia Ruskin University, before you arrive in the UK;

- help you with any problems you may have with your visa, entitlement to work, accommodation, health, money and tuition fees;

- provide help with English, if you need it;

- offer you a programme of activities to welcome you to Anglia Ruskin before you start your course, and a calendar of social events throughout the year to help you get the most out of studying with us; and

- give you the latest news and information, and links to other websites, for international students on our website (**www.anglia.ac.uk/iss**).

We expect you to:

- ask us for help as soon as possible if you have any problems;

- give us accurate information when you ask us for help;

- give us proof of your identity, and any other documents we ask you for;

- keep to UK immigration rules and any advice we give you about your visa; and

- take an English Language test and go to English Language classes and workshops if we assess you as needing to do so.

## 4. Other support

We will:

- tell you the outcome of your application to the Access To Learning Fund (ALF) within one week of the deadline for applications;
- pay your ALF payment into your bank account within two weeks of the deadline for applications (if you qualify for help from the ALF);
- give you advice about special-needs assessments and the Disabled Students' Allowance (DSA);
- carry out a detailed assessment of your needs if you have very special needs;
- give you clear information about the level of support we agree with you;
- respond to you within 48 hours if you contact us about counselling (this service is available Monday to Friday, not including bank holidays);
- try to see any student who is extremely upset on the same day as they contact us; and
- make an appointment for you with a careers adviser within five working days, if you ask us to by e-mail (or within seven working days if you contact us by another method).

We expect you to:

- give us proof of your identity and any other documents we ask you for when you apply for financial help;
- give us full and accurate information on application forms and copies of any documents we ask you for;
- keep to any deadlines when you apply for funding;
- tell us, before you start your course, if you have a disability, learning difficulty or an illness;
- make an appointment, before your course begins, to discuss your needs (if you cannot make an appointment before your course begins, contact us as soon as possible);
- tell us if your needs change; and
- ask for our help as soon as you need it – this will help to stop your problem getting worse, and help you to be more independent.

# After you graduate

We will:

- post your final European Diploma Transcript to your home address within five working days of the date of the relevant Awards Board; and
- post your certificate to your home address within eight weeks of the date of the relevant Awards Board.

We expect you to:

- fill in the Destination of Leavers from Higher Education (DLHE) survey shortly after you graduate.

# The sharpest minds need the finest advice.
# **Kogan Page** creates success.

## www.koganpage.com

You are reading one of the thousands of books published by **Kogan Page**. As Europe's leading independent business book publishers **Kogan Page** has always sought to provide up-to-the-minute books that offer practical guidance at affordable prices.

**KoganPage**